The Fickle Widow's Retreat

A Memoir of Mourning and Moving on in Middle Age

MARSHA SAMITT WILCHFORT

Barringer Publishing, Naples, Florida
www.barringerpublishing.com
Cover, graphics, layout design by Lisa Camp
Cover art by Erik Pflueger

ISBN: 987-0-9961973-0-4

Library of Congress Cataloging-in-Publication Data
The Fickle Widow's Retreat / By Marsha Samitt Wilchfort

Printed in U.S.A.

This is a memoir.
All characters, organizations,
and events portrayed in this novel are
products of the author's creativity and memories.

DEDICATION

To Be Nice Bernice, my mother, who loved Ron before I did.
Without Ron, I wandered about in circles and triangles
to form the perfect square.

ACKNOWLEDGMENTS

Hugs and gratitude to Adam and El.
for listening to countless versions of my work.
I would like to thank Roger Rosenblatt for his
generosity, wisdom, and humor.
Thank you, Lou Ann Walker, for sharing your
creativity, spirit, and enthusiasm.
Kaylie Jones, thank you for confusing me
and flunking me (just fooling!).
Alice, thank you for not being *Alice in Wonderland*.

MARSHA SAMITT WILCHFORT

Adam, me. pink dogwood tree

TABLE OF CONTENTS

For better or worse

PROLOGUE

Ron's body stiffened, his skin turned blue, and his three kidneys stopped functioning—the two kidneys he was born with and his transplanted one. He looked upward toward the heavens to a God he did not believe in and died. Two weeks later, I bought a red Mini Cooper that smiled at me with its jaguar-like lights. He had stopped smiling sometime after the stroke.

He was ecstatic about receiving the kidney transplant; he thought he would be finished with dialysis and possibly living a somewhat normal life. Ron had waited five years for the kidney, only to be told he also needed a new heart, or he wouldn't last five years. If he was apprehensive about the surgeries, he never showed it. He wanted to make it easier for me. He just went forward, never complained, and never felt sorry for himself. He knew that self-pity would destroy him.

I called my Mini Cooper "Baby." She was wide, short, and hugged my body. He was long, lean, ill, and now dead. She respected and accommodated my shortness. If I were a car, I'd be a Mini Cooper. If I could cry there would be no stopping.

"Cry me a river, I've cried a river over you," (Written by Arthur Hamilton) only it's not like that at all. If I let go would my tear duct use its allotment of tears? Do they regenerate or degenerate? It's not a crummy starfish. Is there such a thing as drowning in one's tears, rendering them forever depleted so that you can never cry again? Do you lose your heart, too, or just the tear maker? How much does a tear weigh? Are they all the same size, or do they not conform to anything? Could crying become a new weight loss program? It's not a snowflake, though it might as well be. Is crying a physical activity? The loss of salt is tasty. I don't cry in tears.

The future is forever becoming the past. The past lives deep in space and time. I just want it to slow down. When we went to weddings and other affairs, Ron would count the number of people in attendance. He would calculate how much gift money the bride and groom would receive. He wasn't an accountant; he was an attorney. He would go from table to table at affairs having his picture taken. After about six tables and three Bloody Marys, the photographer would say, "You! Get out of this photo." Ron would put his arms around strangers smiling his vodka grin. This became some kind of tradition. When our friends would receive the photos, they were either furious or hysterical, probably both. Ron would be systematically erased through chemicals; his sweet face left at the assigned table.

In the world of me without Ron, I'm a widow, as was my grandmother before me at the same age—fifty-five...

1

CHARLESTON CHEWS

It was August of 2004 and Ron died May 17, 2003. I was in possession of Ron's AAA card. I was fifty-five going on twenty-two. I made plans for a road trip away from Long Island in "Baby," my new, red Mini Cooper. It was summer with light clothes, endless light, and beach-like breezes. This was my first solo sojourn. Ten pages of maps, freeways, and highways sat by my side as I headed to Charleston, South Carolina. My AAA membership was invaluable. This trip was not to be anything like *On the Road*: there wouldn't be sex, drugs or Jack Kerouac. I brought show tunes for the CD player. I wanted to go somewhere that we never visited. Charleston was 836 miles from home, and I'd never been there. I stuffed two large suitcases with summer clothes. I figured that when I ran out of clothes, the trip would be over. It could be a week, or two or three.

Ron's clothes hung in the closet in the house in Westhampton. My clothes were in the trunk. His wallet, keys, and ID were in his night-table drawer in the off chance that he might need them.

I set the alarm for five a.m. I was in the shower at four a.m. I couldn't sleep. I wasn't sure if it was excitement or fear. Dawn came. I liked the peacefulness of an early morning in the car, so I could witness the first light. I made a hotel reservation at a Holiday Inn in Mt. Pleasant, South Carolina, about five miles from downtown Charleston.

I left the house. I locked the door with my maps all waiting to be used. I got into the car. I had all the food I needed. I backed out slowly and never looked back. I remembered that kid game: "He loves me; he loves me not." He's dead. He can love me all he wants, but I hate him for dying, for being sick, and for being brave. His clothes should be in the trunk with mine. He should have driven us out of New York. I used to drive in the rural farm areas. You know the unsaid rituals of relationships, the roles we play. The roles were done.

I cannot listen to the music he liked: Paul Simon, Neil Diamond, and Barry Manilow. I thought he had awful taste in music with the exception of Paul Simon. We were night and day in our musical tastes. I found solace in music. Most of the music I listened to was in a foreign language. I didn't need the words; the instruments spoke to me. *Fado* music was the music of Portugal. It was melancholy, which is my new middle name. I made the trip in one day. There was nothing else to do.

My status has changed. People treat me differently without a husband. I have become invisible to some and a threat to others. I have become my own friend. Be Nice Bernice is what I called my mother. She read the "Arts and Leisure" section of the *Sunday Times* religiously; I do too.

Ron and I would divide the paper. I would take "Arts and Leisure," "Book Review," "Style," "Week in Review," "Real Estate," and, of course, the magazine section. Ron would take "News," "Sports," more sports, and stocks.

I submitted an essay for the back page of the *New York Times* and received a personal rejection, as well as a rejection from the *New Yorker.* I saved them. Ninety percent of the pieces published on the back page of the *Times* are from published writers. The odds weren't good. I wrote a piece explaining to them why my piece did not get in. I did not send it to them.

Two weeks earlier, my cousin, Ellen, taught me how to pump gas. She wrote the following list:

Make sure you know what kind of gas you require
Know where your gas tank is
Open gas tank
Sometimes the lever of the tank has to be pushed up
Choose the price of gas now
Pump till it stops pumping
Replace the cap on your gas tank
Keep hand sanitizer in the car
Remember to remove your credit card
You will no doubt thank me for this.

I wanted to kill her because she made me feel so incompetent. She also wanted to show me how cruise control worked. I declined the offer.

I was cruising on Route 27 and headed toward the Southern State Parkway to central Long Island and then to Queens. I passed the exit to the first home Ron and I purchased. The three of us lived there for eighteen long years, give or take a year. I felt nothing. It made me think of the song "Nothing" in *A Chorus Line.* I passed some of the Queens apartments that we lived in as a young married couple with a gorgeous little boy who looked like Etan Patz, the six-year-old boy who went missing in 1979 in New York City and ended up on a milk carton. Sometimes when we were in the city, people stared at Adam. We were healthy; life was simpler.

Ron and his Mona Lisa tie

Ron was a bit shy of six feet with fair skin and a few freckles on his face. His auburn hair warranted the freckles. His hair was usually uncombed unless he was making a court appearance. He was 180 pounds when he was young. He was suited up for court and looked lawyerly and handsome. He looked hot when he wore a certain shade of teal blue. His eyes were green on alternating Fridays. I am five feet two. I weighed ninety-two pounds when we married. My hair was a boring shade of mousy brown that hung down my back. I smoked cigarettes and consumed large amounts of dark chocolate before it was healthy. Ron thought I was beautiful; I thought he was funny. He liked making people laugh. He could be the center of attention, if it suited him.

The Southern State Parkway becomes the Belt Parkway in Brooklyn. The Belt Parkway has a lovely view of the water and the joggers but if I glanced at the water; I'd surely crash. Normally, there were at least two accidents per hour with traffic jams of one to two hours. The winding road was all part of New York, New York. My gas tank was full. *Can-Can*, the musical, was playing on my CD player:

"Everyman is a stupid man, a stupid man; a stupid man everyman is a stupid man except the man you love." (From *Can-Can* the musical by Cole Porter)

I loved this song and found myself singing along. My French accent was *très bonne. Please*, I thought, *no accidents here.* I was losing myself in music.

Gwen Verdon became a star after her performance in *Can-Can.* I met her in a coffee shop in Westhampton. I walked up to her; she was seated at the counter drinking tea. I told her she was my mother, Be Nice Bernice's, favorite singer and dancer. I was wearing an old, leather aviation jacket that belonged to Adam. He grew. I didn't. I inherited it. She grabbed my jacket and said she adored it. I asked her if she wanted it. She smiled at me and said no. She apologized to me for not looking so great; she had a cold.

My plan was to pump gas, pee, and eat the sandwiches that were in the cooler in one day. My goal was to be efficient. I ejected the *Can-Can* CD and inserted Warren Zevon who died around the time Ron did. At Ron's funeral, I gave out the words to one of Warren Zevon's last songs titled "Keep Me in Your Heart." Warren died of sex, drugs, and rock n' roll, or lung cancer. Ron died of everything except cancer. I was sure, if Ron lived a bit longer, that cancer would be on the list.

I used a Clinique makeup bag as my change purse. There were many things I didn't care about. I deposited the change on a daily basis into the change purse. It was loaded. I kept a twenty in it as well. I was hungry, I needed gas, and I had to pee. I was on the lookout for the next station with a determined nervousness that I might pee in my pants. It was lousy planning on my part. I was relieved to find a station. Instead of inserting my card, I thought it would be economical to get rid of my change. Less is more, sometimes. I wore sloppy, comfy clothes: a tee shirt, jean shorts, and my straw hat was in the empty seat next to me. I was of the opinion that I needed thirty dollars' worth of gas. When I entered the station, I peed first. I was grateful for small things. I didn't have to use an outside toilet with a key that failed to lock the door.

For better or worse

Things were going my way. I walked in, keyless, and did my business. I walked toward the gentleman behind the counter. I had my green, Clinique change purse in my hand. I probably had more makeup than time left to use it.

The man said, "I am Farouq. What can I do for you?" I was hoping he would pump the damn gas, but I knew better.

"Hi," I said. "I'd like thirty dollars of the cheapest fuel on number three. Would it be OK if I gave you change?" I think I was the only one in the place that was not using a debit card. No one was behind me, so I didn't feel terrible about putting my coins on the counter to count. Farouq smiled. His shiny, shaved, bald head made me think of Yul Brynner as the King of Siam

They sold fruit candy, gifts, beer, soda, and ice cream. You might have thought you were in a deli or a pharmacy. Everything was for sale— batteries, maps, hair products. His smile made me think that he thought we were of the same tribe. I was not surprised. I am of the opinion that I am an Eskimo, and my parents purchased me at a discount at E.J. Korvettes in New York. The three of us frequented that store on many occasions for bargains.

Farouq interrupted my thoughts, "Are you Arabic, miss?"

He's right. I am a miss. I smiled at him, not flirty but not innocent. He said I could begin pumping. I had $52.57 in cold coins.

A young black man walked in and asked Farouq for one condom. I didn't know they sold them loose. I remembered that Ron's came in a package. I never knew where he purchased them. I was not with him when he did.

My grandfather owned a deli in Manhattan. They sold many of the same items as a convenience store. They sold cigarettes loose, like they did at the City Lights Bookstore in San Francisco where the Beat generation hung out. My grandmother also worked in the store. They lived in an apartment in the building where the deli was. When she was a young girl, my mother worked in her father's store. Be Nice Bernice, my mother, and the bread-slicing machine had an accident. She sliced a piece of her index finger. That was the end of her hand-modeling career. She looked like Hedy Lamarr; my father looked like a cross between Montgomery Clift and Johnny Depp.

I was done pumping gas. I needed only twenty-seven dollars and walked back into the store. The kid buying the condom was still there. I asked Farouq to give the change he owed me to the condom kid. You can never have too much safe sex. I looked back; I saw Farouq motion to the kid to gather the change. I was back on the road.

On one of my numerous gas, pee, and food stops, I was pumping gas and getting cocky because I was getting the hang of it. I hated pumping gas. I know it is old school, but shouldn't our husbands pump our gas? Was this why southern women married? Why midwestern women married? One hour out, I realized I had left my AARP credit card in the slot at the pump. I had a list of numbers to call if I lost the card. I had another credit card with me because I knew this would happen. Is this pumping gas routine supposed to be easier? You don't have to pump gas in New York unless you want to.

I was entering South Carolina because the sign said, "Welcome to South Carolina."

I was looking for Route 17 after exiting I-95, I-20 E, and I-520. It was one lane going south and one lane going north. The sky had been bright and clear all day through many states. I was not sure how many miles were left. Although the daylight was with me, the sky was turning dark and it was only four p.m. I had plenty of gas. A flash of lightning—it was about to rain on my parade. I clutched the steering wheel as if my hold would soften the rain. The windshield wipers did little. The wipers were good for little baby rains but not torrential thunderstorms. My Baby and I could not get off the road. There were no exits. I remembered when I was a kid that Be Nice Bernice hid under her bed when there was lightning and thunder. I turned the CD player off.

This was a storm. In the south when it rains, you need to turn your lights on. I stared straight ahead at the lights of the car in front of me. Most cars passed me by and gave a honk to let me know I was driving too slowly. I knew that. The vegetation that I saw was beginning to take on that beach-like flora that I loved. Most of the license plates were from Georgia and South Carolina. The cars whizzed right past me. My hands were like Siamese twins connected to the steering wheel. Surgery might be needed to free me from the wheel.

Ron and I were coming back from the Talkhouse in Amagansett. We saw Buster Poindexter perform "Hot Hot Hot." I was the designated driver, as Ron had too much to drink. Montauk Highway was a one-way in and one-way out road like Route 17. I was a slow driver at night, even sober. Everyone was honking at me. I was close to tears since there was no place to pullover.

I heard a siren. I knew it was for me. I composed myself; Ron told me I was driving too slowly. I pulled over, and the police officer asked us where we were coming from. I said the Talkhouse. He asked to see my hand. They stamp your hand when you go into the place. He knew I was telling the truth.

He said, "I know you have not been drinking, but do you know you were holding up traffic for miles on Montauk Highway? Someone called to report it."

"I wanted to be careful because the deer were everywhere. They just dart out when you least expect it," I responded.

"You were driving fifteen to twenty miles under the speed limit. I'll let you go, but please increase your speed; it's dangerous to drive too slowly."

I said thank you. I drove away. By the time this little detour was over, no one was behind me. I drove a bit faster.

Ron was laughing. "You almost got a ticket for not speeding. Only you, Marsha."

I think I am getting close to the hotel in Mt. Pleasant.

My fifty-five-year-old legs were cranky and creaky. They wanted out. I saw the hotel from the car. I exited left. Then I lost the hotel or at least sight of it. The rain didn't help. My eyeglasses were fogging up. I called the hotel on my cell. I hoped they could walk me through this. It was past eight p.m. I needed half a Xanax.

Sometimes, before I left the house in Westhampton, I did errands that did not need to be done. I sat in the Mini Cooper that I purchased two weeks after Ron cruised away from me. I listened to the message on the answer machine, the sweet voice telling callers we were not home. I called it frequently. His friends told me it disturbed them. That is what I have left. I have even called it when I am in the house. It calms me. I called it now. I fell in love with Ron's voice as a young woman.

I told the receptionist at the hotel I had a reservation and was near them but had lost my way with the rain and all.

"Please do not give my room away in case I don't show up by nine p.m." The man said OK and asked me where I was. If I knew where I was, then I wouldn't be calling you. I was near a salad bar restaurant. He asked me if I saw iron gates. I told him I did not see any iron gates. We were disconnected. I called back—same lucky guy.

"I'm sorry, but I don't see iron gates." He said that Iron Gate Boulevard was near the salad bar restaurant, and I should go straight and make a right on Hungry Neck Boulevard. The hotel was on the right. I saw the hotel. I felt great.

The stiffness in my calves gave away my age. My baby legs still look good, but they don't move with the agility of a younger me. My shorts were crinkled; my shirt had ketchup stains on it, but no one cared or was looking. I parked the car. I stretched a bit. I loaded my suitcases on the luggage rack.

I found my room. I did not unpack or take my pills. I unhooked my bra, took off my shorts, and slept in my tee shirt like a college kid or Jack Kerouac. I called my son, Adam, and told him I was in South Carolina and would speak to him in the morning.

I couldn't get up to turn off the lights. Sleep came quickly. I heard the phone ring. Is it a dream? I tried to answer the phone and as I opened one eye, it occurred to me that nothing was ringing. This happened at least three to four times a night wherever I was when I was sleeping. What was the difference between an auditory hallucination or a dream, a memory? I woke again and the lights were on. For a nanosecond I thought I was in Westhampton in my large bedroom, in the king-sized bed. Three illegal, alien gardeners could be in the bed and I would not know it.

I slept on the edge of the bed in a fetal position. It was dark outside. I unpacked my clothes. It seemed like a strange collection of clothes. I don't remember what I packed. I took a shower. The water felt great. I rid myself of yesterday. Light was peeking in the window. I was clean, hungry, and wide awake; breakfast was in the lobby. My hair was wet. I was reading my complimentary copy of *USA Today*. The hotels must get a special deal on the newspaper; they all have them.

There were business people, families, assorted travelers, and journeymen here. Where was everyone going? I ordered my breakfast of French toast and coffee. It was raining again. I decided to take a ride and see what Mt. Pleasant was like. I already knew it was hot and humid.

I passed small lean-to huts where the African American women wove baskets in the rain. Every half mile was another little hut. I stopped at the first one where a small, plump woman was working while wearing a red, cotton, flowery dress with a little lace on the sleeves.

She said, "Hi, would you like a peach?" It was drizzling. She was barefoot, and I was curious about how unaffected she was by the weather with no shoes. I said yes to the peach and thanked her. I looked at her baskets. I love baskets. One more and I would be a basket case. I bought four, all different from each other. She said she would take ten dollars off since I purchased four. She gave me a big smile and a large bag for my four baskets.

Her people were probably slaves on the rice plantations on the coast of South Carolina and Georgia. I didn't bargain with her. I believe the less you have, the more you give. Her name was Selsa.

Later, I traveled on the same road. I noticed The Mount Pleasant Regional Library was only a turn away. It was perfect for light summer reading; dark winter reading. I stayed in the library for an hour. I liked being surrounded by books.

The Westhampton Beach Library had an annual book sale. They sell donated books from estates and personal libraries. It was held in the summer when the crowds of vacationers and summer people congregate on Main Street. I love libraries and bookstores. I also liked to read the inscriptions that were written inside the books. I have been to this library sale numerous times. I was roaming around aimlessly. The librarians and staff attempted to organize the books with some kind of logic, some books were still in boxes. There was an abundance of reading material.

I was in a small room with poetry books. I noticed a large red book. It was the collected works of Allen Ginsburg on sale for a dollar. I bought it and returned home with my treasure. It was signed! I found some of Ginsberg's poetry interesting. *Kaddish* was one of Allen Ginsberg's poems. It is a prayer for the dead in Judaism to remember those who passed away. Allen wrote *Kaddish* in memory of his mother, Naomi Ginsberg, who died in 1956. His mother suffered from schizophrenia. Allen drew a large doodle of a monster with the words "TYGER! TYGER!" above the doodle from "The Tyger," William Blake's poem. I didn't bring any reading material with me to Charleston. It was not that kind of trip.

I made a donation to the library and asked the librarian to purchase books for their shelves that Ron would have liked to read, based on Ron's reading history. I never asked her which specific books were purchased; I knew they were about history, current events, and politics. I didn't want to know what books Ron wasn't able to read. I felt like a book, opening a page a day at a time. It was not familiar. No one knew me. I didn't know anybody. The anonymity was a blessing; I would reinvent myself. Everyone lies. Do Buddhists lie? I lied.

I awoke; it was dusk. I had missed lunch. The hotel was on Hungry Neck Boulevard. I felt dusky and hungry. It's raining; I took a shower. I put on makeup, jeans, and a black blouse. Maybe I wore too many clothes for Charleston in August. I drove down a street with numerous eating places. I found a parking spot. The rain followed me. I parked in front of an Irish pub—I heard pubs have good food. I decided to sit at the bar. It was neither overly crowded nor noisy. The bartender did what he was supposed to do.

"I would like a Chardonnay and a glass of water, please." He brought me a menu. I knew what I wanted—a well-done burger with fries.

The Chardonnay made me feel mature. Here I was alone in a new city at a bar, just me and my Chardonnay. The sound of the rain hitting the roof of the pub made me feel secure. I had never been in a bar by myself. There was a couple on a date in their mid-thirties, a couple of men in their forties, and three single women. Seated a few seats away from me was a man, alone for now. I sipped my drink and water. I waited for dinner.

My cremated burger arrived and I cut it in half; it can get sloppy with all the ketchup I put on it. I turned the ketchup bottle upside down to drip on my deadly burger. I was told that if it was Heinz brand, you touch the '57' on the side of the bottle and it "goops" out--but not today. The man I spotted before smiled at me and asked if he could help. I said sure. He moved to the empty seat next to me with his beer. He had the touch; the ketchup was ready to slide onto my plate.

"Thank you," I said. "I don't think I could have eaten my burger without the ketchup." We introduced ourselves.

"Do you live here, Bob?"

"Yes and no, I am here on assignment. I live on Andros Island in the Bahamas.

"Year round?"

"Most of the year. I lived in Jacksonville on and off until my wife died."

"I am sorry. I killed my husband; he wasn't behaving."

We both laughed out of awkwardness. I let him know that I, too, was a widow. The things that we tell strangers, we don't tell our loved ones. It was nothing but madness.

"I have a day off tomorrow. Would you like to go to Charleston?"

"Yeah, that would be fine," I said. I was going to go today. Bob asked me where I was staying. He said he was at the Marriott which was a two-minute walk from my hotel. He said he would pick me up at eleven a.m.

"See you then," I said. Driving back to the hotel, I realized I was going on a date.

I set the alarm for nine a.m. and slept soundly. Bob was about five feet ten and wore a baseball hat. He had more hair in the little ponytail than on his head.

My father and I became a widow and a widower within three months of each other. I think that is the extent of what we have in common. At eighty-two, my father went to a dance and called me up before he left. He was petrified; he threw up on his fancy clothes.

I was curious about Charleston and Bob. Ellen, my cousin, mentor, and crazy person who taught me how to pump gas and tried to teach me cruise control, suggested that I buy condoms. I listened to her. It took close to a week until I actually acquired the condoms.

I think I'm allergic to latex.

When I was married, we didn't use lubricants. I asked Ron to buy sanitary napkins for me when I was cramping. He was not at all happy about that chore. He thought he was some kind of hero. He had purchased Depends. I wanted to slap him.

I was walking down the condom lubrication aisle in Rite Aid. The store had so many choices, so little time: Trojan Ecstasy, Trojan Extended Pleasure, Durex, and Lifestyles Pleasure. They came in various sizes. Durex Non-Latex was the right choice.

I slipped the condoms in my pocketbook. What if I am stopped or arrested? Senior citizen widow shoplifting condoms. I can see it now. I was a condom kleptomaniac. What if there was a picture of me on the store camera? What will Adam think? When I got back to the hotel, I hid them somewhere in my medication bag. I was going on a date—a day trip to Charleston.

The dance, "The Charleston," was named for the city of Charleston. The candy, Charleston Chews was created in 1922, it was also named for the dance. Josephine Baker danced the Charleston at the *Folie Bergere* in Paris in 1926. I clicked on YouTube and wrote Josephine Baker Charleston. Viola... She danced the Charleston ...the footage was from 1926...preserved on YouTube.

Would Miss Baker be pleased to know that anyone with a computer could visit with her on YouTube? It was a treat. I had a feeling Ron would be "YouTubing" the Beach Boys, Neil Diamond, and Paul Simon. Josephine Baker did a banana dance with fake fruit. Can you imagine if she used fresh fruit that was flapping on her waist? Lady Gaga's meat costume was a poor imitation of a one-of-a-kind legend. Is it possible there was nothing original left to do? How about residing in outer space?

I'll take a one-way ticket.

Bob arrived at my hotel at eleven a.m. We drove over the brand-new, steely, sleek Arthur Ravenel Jr. Bridge. Charleston was in view, moss was everywhere, and I felt light and airy. The sky was commanding. It welcomed you to the city. The water wrapped you in like an infant, protected and free.

The 59th Street Bridge in New York has been falling apart for years. Yellow cabs contrast the gritty grunge of the bridge; the sky hides from view out of embarrassment. New York was a noise machine.

He parked the truck. We walked around the indoor and outdoor market on East Bay Street. They had crafts, food, and maple-sugared pecans. I will come back here alone. We strolled around for forty-five minutes or so. We were protected from the sun. Bob asked if I was hungry. The aroma of the chocolate and sugary pecans increased my appetite.

I wanted maple-sugared pecans for lunch, but we made our way over to a bar and restaurant. I was sure there were more interesting places but this was fine. We sat at the bar. Bob ordered a Coors and I ordered a Chardonnay.

He told me his wife Jackie died two years ago. She was his second wife. He didn't have children. He had a contract with the government on Andros Island in the Bahamas. I told him I was in the Bahamas light years ago. I asked if he went to the casinos. He told me that as an employee on the island, he was not allowed to gamble. I didn't know that. It made sense. He ordered a burger and I ordered a grilled chicken sandwich. I had a little buzz. He ordered another beer. I asked for a glass of water. His ponytail was salt and pepper. His fries looked good. Since I didn't order the sugary treats, I asked him if I could have a fry so he put a bunch on my plate. His second beer appeared as I was nursing my Chardonnay.

Bob lived in Jacksonville, Florida, when he was not on contract with AUTEC, the US Navy's Atlantic Undersea Test and Evaluation Center. It sounded like submarine secrets to me. He paid the check. I thanked him. I asked if we could split it. He said no. We headed back to the truck. I took a picture of the bridge with his camera. In the truck, he handed me a bag and it smelled like heaven. I opened it and discovered the pecans.

"How sweet of you, Bob, thank you." He must have purchased it on one of my bathroom trips. We were nearing Mt. Pleasant; he asked me if I wanted to go back to my hotel.

"We can go to my hotel, I have a suite," he said.

"Sure." We drove in silence. His suite had a kitchen, sitting area, and bedroom. He turned the TV to CNN.

"Marsha, care for a beer?"

"I think I will have a nut. Care for one?" He had his beer and I had my sugar. I sat on the couch next to him. He looked toward me. He kissed me, tender and slow. My hand was on his thigh. He unsnapped my bra. I took it off. I undid his belt. His mouth was warm; we kissed with long, noisy kisses. I was on top of him. He touched my breasts. My nipples pointed in arousal. I felt his manhood against me. He removed my jeans; he was on top of me. He produced a condom and entered me. He teased; he was in me and then pulled out, creating tension and almost pain. He was strong; he could lift me and turn me. I was flexible. He was hard. He was in again and the rhythm was right. Our breathing was changing, panting. There was nothing else; bodies joined in connecting, concentrating, and irritating pain that was pleasure. The breathing shifted, slowing down. I heard cars driving past the hotel. On CNN, some politician was caught with his pants down. We lay down in our sweat. I was relaxed. I went to the bathroom. I saw Cialis on the counter. It could have been Viagra. I noticed that vagina and Viagra are different by one letter. No

25

coincidence with Niagara or Viagra Falls. I would love to name drugs for the pharmaceutical companies.

I thought about the differences in our anatomies. I wanted to go back to my room. He was resting. I got dressed. I laid down beside him and whispered in his ear that I was going to my place. He told me he was working tomorrow and asked if I wanted to get together for dinner. I gave him my cell phone number. I walked back to the hotel. I thought of Eartha Kitt singing "I want to be evil. I want to be bad. I want to wake up with that dark brown taste," written by Raymond Taylor and Lester Judson. I wanted to take a shower though I liked the smell of him and the taste.

When I woke the next day, I felt a walk on the beach coming on. Isle of Palms was not far at all. The sky hugs you, the water surrounds you, the clouds drift, and the sand sticks to your toes. You can take sloppy, comfortable steps, free of shoes or office confines—me and a grain of sand. It was a pedicure.

The Isle of Palms is a barrier island with a population of four thousand people. I walked for over an hour. Sullivan's Island was nearby but today was beach day. I ate lunch at Poe's Tavern where the burgers carried the names of his poems. Annabelle Lee was indeed a burger. I ordered a regular burger light on the ketchup, heavy on the melancholy. There is also a Library named after him on Sullivan's Island.

I spent another evening with Bob. He was leaving for a few days. He hoped to see me when he returned to Mt. Pleasant.

The following day I took the bridge to Charleston. I wanted to roam around the city. There were numerous streets with the usual stores: Gap, Banana Republic, Chico's, and White House/Black Market. There was a cemetery with moss drooping and touching gravesites. The gray moss and marble created a black-and-white photo that was moody and lovely. I wanted to take a picture. I had lunch in a French restaurant that did not have tables, just counters in a horseshoe. The brie sandwich and fruit on a baguette was tasty. I found my way again to the indoor and outdoor market.

There was a black woman who was making brown-faced dolls in her space. She painted eyes, noses, and mouths on their faces. Her name was Mae. I told her my name was Marsha. The dolls were dressed in colorful fabric with flowery prints. Mae told me she used to make costumes for the theater. I was not surprised; her workmanship was impeccable. She was eighty-two years old and her eyes were not as good as they used to be, so she makes these small dolls.

I told her my grandmother's name was also May but spelled differently. My grandmother sewed. She embroidered a tablecloth for all of her grandchildren's weddings. She told me each of the dolls' names. They were six inches tall. I picked up a doll in a lavender dress with a paisley print. I loved the color with the brown face. The name of the doll was Edith.

My mother's sister's name was Edith, Ellen's mother. Mae let me know that the dolls were named for documented slaves. I purchased the Edith doll. My Aunt Edith married a rich man who had tobacco plants in Cuba. My aunt had live-in help. The woman who took care of things was Willie Mae. I used to tremble when I visited my aunt because we were poor and they were not. Willie Mae wore a white uniform in the breakfast room. In the formal dining room, Willie Mae wore a black uniform with a white apron. My aunt had a bell to ring when she needed Willie Mae.

The dining room had a couch in it. I thought couches were for living rooms. There was a doll dressed in a deep-cranberry, light-green, and floral print. Her name was Bernice, as in Be Nice Bernice, my mother. I purchased her as well. I was happy and spooked. I told Mae it was a pleasure to meet her. I hoped to see her again when I went downtown.

The next time I went to the market, she was nowhere to be found. I read about a restaurant in Shem Creek with a live band. I knew I would not be dancing the Charleston, but I liked live music. I arrived at the restaurant and was asked by the hostess how many were in my party. I told her that there would be no party, just a table for one please. I wondered if I would be seated near the kitchen, near the rear of everything. I didn't care. A seat was a seat. I ordered salmon and a glass of Riesling. The band was setting up. It was a large space. If I worried that I might be the only woman seated at a table, I might never go out.

The salmon was tasty; the Riesling was a nice pairing with the fish. I decided to sit at the bar. I ordered another Riesling. There was a couple seated at the bar with an empty chair next to the man. I sat down next to him. They were older. I don't think I look my years. When I was younger, I was able to judge a person's age to near perfection. The man was older than the woman. He smiled and asked me about my day. "Fine," I said. The woman—a blond dressed smart but simple—pretty much said it all. She glanced my way and introduced herself to me. Her name was Charlotte. She asked me where I was from. I told her I was on vacation. I asked them if they were on vacation, but I knew by their accent that they were not. They appeared to be on the second rounds of drinks. Charlotte switched seats with Bill. I was thinking it was because she was petrified I might steal her husband.

I was an introverted-extrovert and Charlotte sensed that. She told me she has a married son, two grandkids, and a daughter-in-law that they were not happy about. I was shocked and bewildered that people everywhere have issues with their in-laws. What was true from where I was from was also true here.

Charlotte and Bill owned a furnished, three-bedroom condo on the Isle of Palms. It was a hop, skip, and a jump to the ocean. There was a view of the sunrise every day unless it rained.

"Our son doesn't know that we own this. We didn't want her [the daughter-in-law] to find out."

"Charlotte, do you ever rent it out?"

"We did that; we are trying to avoid a broker fee." I asked if I could look at it; I was interested in renting it for January, February, March, and, maybe, April. Bill and Charlotte wrote the address on a paper napkin. We decided to meet that Saturday at noon. I placed the paper napkin in my wallet. I was excited about viewing the apartment. We said our goodbyes

Would they show up on Saturday? They had numerous drinks; people drink. The paper napkin was the telling fact. I had notepads everywhere except in my pocketbook. Nonetheless, I found the condo on the Isle of Palms. I waited for about forty-five minutes but they never showed, even after I called them on their cell phone.

Even though I had clothes left, the trip was over. I was going home to Westhampton. I was looking forward to the drive—just me, no detours. Boring roads and ramp exits lay ahead. I packed and showered. It was easier to go home without any choices needing to be made: whatever was in the closet was placed in the suitcase.

Was it always easier to leave? Not really. Nothing was easy. Nothing was hard. It was a turn in the road—ramps on and off. I left the hotel at eight a.m. It was a sunny day. I had my dolls and baskets. I wondered where they would reside in my house.

2

DOCTORS, DIARIES, BLOOD TESTS, AND DIALYSIS

The drive was easier going home. I was tired, but it felt good to be going home where nothing was expected of me. It seemed like I had been gone for a month, but it was only twelve days, not counting drive time. I resisted the urge to call the house phone and hear Ron's sweet voice. I could make a detour, but I knew I wouldn't. If I wanted to, I could listen to the messages that Ron left me on the phone while he was in the hospital, recuperating from the stroke and the paralysis. He was in a coma for ten days. I held his hand and fussed with his hair. I told him I loved him and it was time to wake up and enjoy this crazy new kidney. He needed a shave.

Eyes closed fingernails long
Beard grows red and grey
Like the dead but not dead
No food no hunger
This is a coma
I pray today
Will be the day
He wakes
He sees
He is back

"Hi, Marsha, you must be seeping [He couldn't say sleeping]. I can call you." Ron hung up and immediately called me back. This would go on until he fell asleep in the hospital. He spoke like a child when he awoke from his coma after the stroke.

"Hi Marsha, you must be in the shower. I can call you." Ron's speech matched a ten-year-old's excitement, after he hit a home run. The fact that he was able to call me without assistance was amazing to him. Apparently, the only activities he thought I did were shower and sleep.

Ron, I thank you for making those recorded messages. I have listened to them more than I should admit. I stopped in Maryland and was on the road again to be home by early evening. My big on shabby, small on chic bedroom awaited me. The clothing choices I had to make for the trip took time, but now I didn't have to make any choices or take any extra time. I just put what was hanging in the drawers and closets in the hotel back in the suitcases.

I hung the clothes in my closet. I stored the empty suitcases in Ron's bedroom. This was what I did post-kidney transplant, post-heart valve replacement, post-coma, and post-stroke. He was gone.

I remembered his first depression. I thought Ron wanted a divorce. He didn't talk to me. He stopped eating and lost thirty pounds. He looked like a Holocaust survivor and I felt like one. His clothes were falling off. He slept all day and at night he cried. I wanted to make his pain go away. I didn't know much about his depression then. I didn't know much about depression. My father's sister suffered from severe episodes of depression. She was hospitalized and Be Nice Bernice told me it was because she was selfish. She told me if I was selfish I, too, would be depressed.

I drove him to the courthouse, if he had a case on the calendar. He talked about suicide. I went to a therapist and was given a name of a psychiatrist. He was given a medication called imipramine. He began to get back his smile, style, humor, and appetite. We told Adam who was nine years old that his father's back went out.

Ron told me that he felt incredible sadness when President Kennedy died. He hiked for hours throughout Queens without eating, hoping to walk away the blues.

It took six months for Ron to recover from the depression. Life began to brighten a bit. I always felt it lurking in a corner, waiting to pop up uninvited, capable of breaking and entering our space and our lives at a moment's notice. The hollow that Ron lived through became the hollow that I feared. I did not feel the same about us. I now lived with the knowledge that Ron could disappear for months without ever leaving the house. I didn't know how many years in total were lost to depression, but it was considerable.

Routines were re-established and life was better. When Ron was forty, he went for a physical with the local internist. He ordered blood tests. On the return visit, Dr. Gluck told him that his blood sugar was high. He thought Ron would be able to control the sugar numbers with an improved diet, but Dr. Gluck did not know Ron's love for ice cream.

He lovingly called me the food police and swallowed all the ice cream and fries he wanted. I found dried-up fries in his jacket pockets. There were times when I made dinner and he didn't eat. I was surprised and thought it was my cooking which was dreary. He had snacked before dinner.

Eventually, he needed medication to control the diabetes. He was compliant with that. He swallowed pills for depression and diabetes. When the diabetes continued to progress, more pills were added and, eventually, he required insulin. There were times when his blood glucose number was low and he needed to have something sweet to eat. I purchased glucose tablets for him. If we were out, he would head on over, wobbling and shaking, to the nearest Häagen Daz ice cream store and purchase a vanilla fudge ice cream cone, followed by one more for the road. He told me that he took advantage of those lows to have as much sugar as possible. He was hopeless, but I loved him. He experienced headaches that required long, not accidental naps. He was sluggish but rarely missed his Monday night tennis game with the guys.

On a routine blood test, it was discovered that his cholesterol and triglycerides numbers were climbing to Mount Everest. The doctors took out their pharmacy pads the moment he walked in the door. A blood pressure pill was added to his ever-growing regimen. He swallowed and sucked it up, but he never changed his eating habits. He was impulsive and childlike in his choices and in some ways I understood. His mother died of a heart attack at fifty-five. His father had a heart attack at sixty-one.

There were endocrinologists to visit and more blood tests. The hollow version of Ron returned as his depressions returned. The psychiatrist pronounced that after three major clinical depressions, it was standard medical practice to diagnose a person as manic-depressive, also known as bipolar. He began swallowing lithium three times a day. The lithium caused tremors in his hands which affected his tennis game. He was competitive, and he took the meds religiously. It was hard for an atheist.

A new word was added to his vocabulary, creatinine, a muscle byproduct and an indicator of kidney health. The test for creatinine in his blood came back elevated. This translated into doctors wanting to see him every three months. He was very popular. Everybody wanted to see him frequently to poke him in the arm and take his blood.

One day they took his blood in the hospital and decided he had a heart attack. He had triple bypass surgery since two arteries were ninety percent blocked, and the third one was thirty percent blocked. Heart problems were genetically predisposed. I supposed that with cautiousness, his heart issues could be controlled. This was true for the diabetes as well but that was not his style.

He had his breastbone and sternum cracked open so they could fix his heart. I was an innocent bystander to his medical nightmares. I was there; I watched as he failed, rallied, and joked. He confused me. His depressions were usually based on an irrational fear that we didn't have enough money.

I thought that if I were him and depressed, I would have curled up in the fetal position because of the serious medical conditions. Maybe then I would have tried to eat better and exercise more. That was not the nature of his medical illnesses. He never exhibited fear over the state of his health, only the fear of his finances, which were not real. Depression, delusions, disease welcome to our world. I recalled the vows, "For better or for worse, in sickness and in health." He healed and went back to work. His law office remained faithful to him, as well as to me. He returned to it as a soldier after battle with his wounds and scars. He had a large scar on his chest which he earned and it healed.

After one of Ron's depressions, I fell apart. I wanted to sleep. I ran out of steam. There was little left of me. I was mentally exhausted. I took a pill for anxiety. I got better and became stronger, end of story. I thank the drug companies. If not for the drug companies—love them or hate them—people with bipolar, depression, and anxiety would be misdiagnosed as schizophrenics and die in mental institutions.

I made a surprise fortieth birthday party for Ron on April 7. I began planning it around the time of the Space Shuttle Challenger tragedy on January 28, 1986. I decided to have the surprise party at our home.

I arranged for Ron's best friend, Phil, and Adam to play tennis while the caterers set up and guests arrived. His sister came in from Arizona. His elderly Uncle Moritz and his wife, Frieda, were there. Sixty friends and family came over to sing and surprise him. He was the perfect person to have a surprise party.

There must have been forty bottles of soda in the basement. He said, "Marsh, why so much soda?" I said they were on sale and that made sense to him. He arrived home smelling tennis and triumphant. There must have been thirty-five cars lined up in our cul-de-sac but he never connected the dots. There were lots of presents, lots of food, lots of friends, and life was good. I made a surprise forty-eighth birthday party for him as well. It was a good idea since on his fiftieth, he was hospitalized somewhere.

At some point after the triple bypass surgery, his blood tests revealed high levels of protein in his urine. He was referred to a nephrologist, a specialist for kidney disorders. We went to the kidney doctor. He performed more blood tests. Ron's blood type was O, the universal donor, but mine was type A, so I couldn't give him my kidney.

The doctors had a practice like Ron's law practice. Everyone was trying to get it right. They practiced daily on folks like him and me. On Fridays, they played golf and practiced their shots. The kidney doctor recommended a biopsy to find out the cause of his elevated numbers. They did a biopsy on Ron's kidney at North Shore University Hospital.

Dr. Salisbury, the kidney doctor, said, "I have good news and bad news." *You just stuck a giant needle in Ron's kidney; he was bleeding cranberry-colored blood. Was he practicing his stand-up comedy routine or was I weary, on the verge of teary?"*

The good news was that Ron's problem kidney was not related to the diabetes. The bad news was that it was idiopathic, which is a fancy term in medical speech saying "I don't know what the hell is wrong with this guy's kidney."

It was explained that it could have been something as simple as having strep throat as a kid and not being treated with antibiotics. I stopped believing they just practiced for money and grants. Ron stopped bleeding and Dr. Salisbury checked him out, handing me a script for more blood tests. We drove home in silence. I glanced over to see how Ron was doing. I noticed that the IV was still in his arm. He was weak and napping. Nothing surprised me. After all, Dr. Salisbury practiced medicine on him. We were minutes from home, and I left him in the car while I ran into the pharmacy. Bradley, the pharmacist, was a friend of ours. I think we were one of his best customers.

"Bradley, hi, could you take the IV out of Ron's arm?"

"Marsha, slow down. What are you talking about? They left the small IV thing in his arm." Bradley asked if he had the IV pole attached, and I was so mad at him that I wanted to slap him.

"Do you think I would have left with a pole in his arm? It would not have fit in the car."

We attended classes at NSUH hospital in Manhasset to prepare for the day when dialysis would be in Ron's life. It was imminent, but it is science and no one knows when. We were in a classroom with blackboards and erasers. The nurses and doctors explained what it would be like to begin treatment. We were the youngest people there. Ron was wearing a suit because he was an attorney and would be leaving for court when this was over. We drove to the hospital separately. Shortly after the doctor walked in, Ron's pager buzzed and he was in the hallway calling his client. Ron received numerous calls and left the classroom. He was there for only thirteen minutes; it was two hours in length. I went home and Ron went to court.

He was on dialysis treatments shortly after the class. He was anemic, lethargic, sick, and needed a minor procedure to provide access in his arm for the machine to remove the toxins from his body. It was a port to facilitate the dialysis. When Ron's treatments started, he was the new kid on the block so they gave him the least desirable time. They began at 7 p.m. and by 11:30 p.m. he was done. I drove him home, a forty-five minute drive. When we returned to the house, he fell asleep immediately. I was wide awake. I think I am an insomniac. I tossed all night and was drowsy all day. His kidneys decided to take a permanent vacation.

Every day, thousands of people, from infants to the elderly, have been saved by dialysis. They don't know who to thank. They think it is the doctors who invented the machine, which in its early stages resembled a washing machine. It removes the toxins from the patients whose kidneys stopped functioning. Kidneys are complicated: they control blood pressure, hormones, and bones.

The man to thank for having these treatments available to all was Richard Milhous Nixon.

At the height of the anti-war demonstrations in 1970, a young student in his final year of law school marched in Washington against President Nixon's foreign policies. This protester did not know that a comprehensive Medicare package had found its way to the president's desk. The president signed it and it passed. It included free dialysis treatments and transplantation costs covered for the donor and recipient. Thirty years later, this same protester, my husband Ron, would be sitting in a chair hooked up to a kidney dialyzer for five hours a day, three days a week.

I also thought of it as a plane ride to nowhere. The nurses were his stewardesses. The doctor was the pilot. The treatment center was his jet.

They had large machines that beeped continuously. Each patient had their own TV, in front of their treatment chair.

Ron would devour The New York Post in his own, very special way so that no one was able to read the paper after he was done with it. He was a sloppy guy. I was tired most of the time. I figured I must be in menopause or perimenopause: a pause from men with no more babies.

It was the eve of September 11, 2001. That night, Ron was hemorrhaging and fell out of bed. The sound woke me up. I called the ambulance and they brought him to Riverhead Hospital. The staff was glued to the TV. It appeared there was a plane crash at the Twin Towers in lower Manhattan. We went to a wedding there many years ago. I needed a Dramamine in the elevator of the Twin Towers. We were on the top floor of the tower where the affairs and parties were held. The nurses were making space available for the survivors of the crash. All the hospitals in the area were doing the same thing. They overlooked some of the regular patients in favor of giving life-saving treatments. They didn't need to clear that much space at the hospital. Everyone knows someone who was lost, just like every Jew has family in Israel except for me.

St. Luke's was the last hospital he was a patient in before he passed. After two physical therapy sessions, he was admitted to the Intensive Care Unit. It was too stressful for him and his failing heart. One of his physical therapists told me that no rehabilitation facility would accept him. His medications were too expensive and the facility by law is obligated to be responsible for that expense. I said I would pay for the medications, but it still wouldn't be allowed. I was approached by an administrator of the hospital who said they would hire an attorney for me. The attorney would be paid for by St. Luke's Hospital. He would be able to have Ron go on Medicaid through some kind of legal loophole. We would bear no responsibility for the costs associated with his care. Ironically, Ron made good money as an attorney. They were trying to help but I could not accept it. It seemed wrong to me.

Be Nice Bernice died. My father came to New York to be with me and heal from his loss. I went to a few rehabilitation centers and nursing homes with my father. We went to two or three facilities. I looked haggard and people assumed I was his wife, since my dad looked pretty healthy.

"What can we do for Mom?" They meant me. I glared at the woman.

"My mother is gone, my husband is ill, and you should ask people questions before you speak." I went to the ladies' room, so I thought, but it was the men's room. A resident was in the correct sex bathroom with his pants and diaper down, eating a dish of ice cream in a stall with the door open. I was on the cusp of tears for my father and Be Nice Bernice. I apologized to the man who was not sure where he was. I certainly did not know where I was.

My laughter was uncontrollable. I laughed so hard I cried salty, snotty sobs. Maybe it was better for him to eat his dessert in private. I don't know. I found my father flirting and talking to the same woman who was mistaken about who might live here. He was having her guess his age, his not so new pastime.

He was eighty-four and looked younger than me these days. We went to another facility and it stank of dirty diapers. I said to my father, "Let's get some ice cream."

As soon as Ron was home, he asked me, "Marsha, how did you turn this house into a hospital?"

Ron's question will torment me forever. Home to him meant that he was well and life would begin again as it was before. He did not remember much of what happened to him medically. That was a good thing.

Since I was the one waiting on the other side of the door for him, the ambulance drivers deposited him in the hospital bed with his assorted paraphernalia associated with the new life he was not going to have. Like the Hoya Patient Lift which is akin to a fork-lift for humans is functional and humiliating.

Around 4:30 in the afternoon, it was time to check his blood pressure, blood sugar, and feed him. Paulette, the nurse, was hired to make sure he swallowed his shitload of pills. We compartmentalized them into the daily pill holder. The colors are pastels: greens, blues, oranges, pinks, reds, yellow liquids, and solid-quartered halves. To take before food, no food, shake before using… When I was a kid, I would see Be Nice Bernice jumping up and down, following the instructions on the bottle that said to "shake well." He required injections of insulin to fortify the pancreas, to heal the heart that was beyond healing, and stabilize the blood pressure. The anti-rejection pills were used so that the brand-new kidney wouldn't be rejected by his body. Organ rejection, people rejection— organs can reject their new home in an old body.

I had a ramp installed in the garage so I could take Ron out of the house for a walk or get him to doctor's appointments. There would be no more tennis on Monday nights with the guys. I remembered that the doctors at St. Luke's told me I could bring him home before the ramp was completed; however, I wanted everything in order before Ron was home. I wished they would have told me that it just didn't matter. I figured out why it didn't matter much too late. They knew how sick Ron was but no one told me. I was mad at myself. I was mad at the hospital system. If I knew more, then I would have taken him home sooner, much sooner. A friend of Ron's had a colleague who was a psychologist at St. Luke's. He had information about his condition. He told his friend how bleak things were for him in the hospital.

I was on the road back home with wheelchairs and ramps. There were file cabinets cluttering the basement. Thirty years of other people's legal lives lived with me instead of Ron.

That August after my Charleston trip, I had his wheelchair ramp removed. I kicked his wheelchair hard. When it hit the ramp, it rolled sideways in the garage. It was upside-down with the wheels spinning. The wood from the ramp smelled fresh like the woods. I picked the wheelchair off the floor. It weighed more than Ron.

I sat in the chair; it was large and uncomfortable. I was slumped over. I couldn't sit straight. I felt paralyzed and didn't know what to do. I wanted to stay in his chair. I didn't want to go back in the house. While I was in the garage, I found a can of purple paint that we had used to paint the front door of the house. I discovered a screwdriver and pried the paint can open. I painted the ramp purple until there was no paint left. I was tired. It was late. The floor of the garage was speckled with wet paint. I forgot to eat. I was covered in paint.

I flopped into bed. I called the company that built the ramp that is now purple. What will become of it? Maybe they can make a dollhouse out of the wood, something fun for a child or a dog. The paint smelled fresh, like a beginning art project, or a new room being renovated.

LUV

I would rebel if I was the L-word. Love is overrated, x-rated, exaggerated.
In the past when I wrote letters, I lovingly signed them.
Love, Marsh

My love was signed in bold print on occasion cards.
The universe of cell phone owner's confirm their love
throughout Verizon towers.

Love begins as an attraction, it can become a distraction.
In the game of tennis and squash love is zero.
In math zero is a number: sometimes.
In Fiddler on the Roof Zero Mostel played the role of Tevye.
Love Minus Zero is a song by Bob Dylan.

If I could be any word, I would choose kindness in the land of alphabet soup.
Kindness and love are alphabetical neighbors.
If I had to choose between the two in my non-alphabet life.
I would go with Love.

3

SOUTHAMPTON WRITERS' CONFERENCE

I had new friends—friends to go to events or bars with. Ron and I took continuing education classes in writing when we first arrived in Westhampton in 1998. I had a writers' group meet at our house once a week for four sessions. We would then take a break for two weeks. I was writing short pieces that weren't great, but they helped get me through the day. I was pleased if someone laughed in the right place.

Ron was alive for some of the classes. Ron bought a cake for the writers in celebration of the written word. We continued with the classes in our home after he died. I spent many years reading, but I lost interest in reading books. Reading was passive; I felt a desperate need to be an active participant in whatever was out there.

The women who led the group was a freelance writer. She taught the creative writing class at Westhampton Beach High School. Most of the writers in my group that I recruited were from the continuing education classes at the high school. There was Libby, a young woman who grew up in Sag Harbor that attended the continuing education class. She was an attorney but did not practice law; she practiced yoga with a passion. She was a brilliant student who looked exactly like Sandra Bullock. We became friends. I am probably about twenty-five years older than Libby. She told me I had a young soul, and I knew she had an old one. Libby was dating Michael, and I insisted that she invite me to their wedding.

I wanted to embrace other people's happiness. She invited me to the wedding. Her mother's best friend was having a surprise shower for Libby. We were asked to write a memory of something for Libby.

To Libby

Not A Poem, 'Tis A Memory

Of my bridal shower thirty-something years ago, I remember it in its brevity and perfection.

I didn't have one. I am here today at yours, knowing it will be all that mine wasn't and more.

I remember calling you two years ago on a rainy Saturday morning when Ron and I were going to a wedding that evening. I wasn't feeling well; I needed a friend. You met me at the beach bakery on Main Street. You left your warm, Michael bed for me. Ron expected me to attend every function. I was the designated driver. It was a two-hour trip. I knew I was sick. You listened to my tale of woe.

We had cake, or should I say I had cake, and you ordered some healthy, cardboard muffin stuff. I felt better seeing you on that dreary, rainy Mayday. I went to that wedding grateful for your friendship. I thought about how lucky Michael was to have you in his life.

Now it is your shower, your wedding, your day, and Michael's day. I can't wait to be there for you and Michael.

Not a poem, not just a memory

Love, Marsha

They married on the beach in Westhampton in a nondenominational ceremony. We removed our shoes once we were on the beach. A woman married them. She wore a shawl with the symbols of many religions. Was she a shaman?

Libby was serious about writing. She graduated from our little class and enrolled in the MFA program at Southampton College. The campus was on the bay. When I was a senior in high school, I applied to Southampton College as an undergraduate. I was waitlisted and didn't have time to wait. I went to Franklin Pierce College in New Hampshire instead.

Libby was a braniac and did well in school; she told me she had been writing since she was six. I believed her. After a year or so, she suggested I attend the summer writers' conference. I gave it some thought and went for it. It was a highly respected workshop that ran from nine to ten days. Libby was my guide and mentor. I had to submit a sample of my work to show evidence of my writing abilities. I also had to use a computer that I recently purchased. My skills were nonexistent on the computer, and I was questioning my writing skills as well. I struggled and cried frequently.

I wanted to nap to avoid making a decision. I knew I would never forgive myself for missing the opportunity. Yes, I could do writing camp. I can always retreat to the cocoon of foreign music afterwards. Libby told me to register for Roger Rosenblatt's class on the literary essay.

Oh, shit! My recurrent fickleness was by my side; it tortured and defined me. The 2005 Southampton College Writers' Conference ran from July 20 through July 31.

I sat at my new computer to start my writing sample. I would write a sentence and accidentally delete the crummy sentence. I was good at saving money but saving sentences presented challenges that I did not expect. I wrote a few essays. It was maddening. I wrote and rewrote it many times. Some things that I wrote I memorized by accident. I would make one copy.

As if by magic, twenty-two copies fell out of the printer. I couldn't stop the printer; it just printed the same page over and over. In my impatience, I must have pressed print numerous times and it printed. It was supposed to be e-mailed. I didn't know what e-mail meant. I brought my essays to the college and handed them to the administrator. They were amused, perhaps this was the only hand-delivered document they had ever received. They told me I could have e-mailed it online. I said I was in the area so I figured I would drive it by. I kept copies. I felt relief that it was literally out of my hands. I later learned that e-mail was the shortened word for electronic mail. Snail mail was postal mail. I received a letter by snail mail from Southampton that I was accepted into the conference. I was pleased, excited, and nervous. I was elated that I received the acceptance by snail mail and only later realized the reason; I never gave them my e-mail address since I never created one.

On the first day we were given name tags. A barbeque took place from four to six p.m. the same afternoon; they fed us well. The keynote speaker was Frank McCourt. The man could speak for hours about his life, his poverty, and his teaching. I will never forget his explanation of how he washed clothes. He put all his clothes on, lathered up, and took a shower. He removed the clothes layer by layer. Eventually he and his clothing were clean in one not-so-quick swoop. What would Martha Stewart think? Who cared? Later that night, Dar Williams performed. I drank and danced with Marilyn or anyone who would dance with me, otherwise I danced alone. I was lucky I lived thirty minutes from the conference. I drove home and prepared for day two.

Roger's class about the literary essay met every other day, beginning July 21st, for two to three hours. There were maybe fifteen or twenty of us. The ages of the students were younger and older than me. I was fifty-eight. Roger appeared in shorts, a golf shirt, and sandals. It was summertime in the Hamptons—what else do you wear? I wore capris, sandals, a straw hat, and several extra pounds. I was thinking beach, but I was in a classroom— there was no other place that I wanted to be. Roger was tall and fair skinned, not much beach for him, I suspected. He had a warm, mischievous smile. He was handsome and talkative. We settled in.

Roger passed a large photo of John Kennedy campaigning with a pregnant Jackie. The photo was taken September 9, 1960. Jackie gave birth to John Fitzgerald Kennedy on November 25, 1960. After that day campaigning in New York, Jackie's doctor told her no more handshaking until the baby was born. In the photo, Jackie's left hand is openly touching John Kennedy's twisted back. Her right hand was shaking a stranger's hand. John Kennedy was touching another hand. There was a large hand in the upper right corner of the photo. I saw John in silhouette. It was a chain of connections; Jackie looked lighthearted. She was wearing white cotton gloves like my grandmother wore. I had a pair like that once upon a time. She appeared happy, joyful, and almost silly in her large coat, large grin, and big belly. One would never think of Jackie Kennedy looking silly. She was reaching out to shake hands with unknown constituents. John was doing the same but not nearly as animated and joyous. Her coat was white; she was plump and puffy. Was she filled with lightness because she was bringing forth life?

There were posters of John Kennedy lining the streets of New York. It was a black-and-white photo by Cornell Capa. I, too, was happy. I loved black-and-white photos, even though my photographer of choice is Diane Arbus. Each of us in the class was asked to describe what we saw. I was aware of the political life of a candidate. People wanted to touch their candidate. They wanted to be close to him. The man who might govern and hopefully change the world. They will never forget the day they shook Kennedy's hand or touched Jackie's glove. They might embellish the story and tell friends that Jack spoke to them. The elated Jackie was touching and reaching out reciprocal handshakes like the Pope is in town. Ron's first major depression occurred when Robert Kennedy was shot. My past was connected to American history.

I had no one to touch anymore, to touch me, to back into, to lean onto, to bump into, to disagree with, or to make up with. There are no more sloppy kisses, or no one to see an Al Pacino movie with. I am without. I am Marsha, Inc. I go where I have never gone before. I am frightened of dying of boredom. I won't die; Adam has been through enough. I pray to stay alive. I now know that when you say your marriage vows, one of you will die first. I never gave that a moment's thought. I was twenty-three when we married.

Ron was demonstrative on the tennis court, in a court of law, and in bed. I imagined in our later years that he and I would spend time with our imaginary grandchildren. One would look like me and one would resemble him. They would be brilliant, funny, and excellent tennis players. After Ron died, I insisted that Adam go to the doctor. His cholesterol was high. He was prescribed Lipitor, just like Ron. I went to my gynecologist. My cranky, precancerous uterus, cervix, ovaries, and assorted organs needed to be removed. A bilateral, hysterectomy would be performed. In Greek the word for uterus is hysteria. Is that why it is called a hysterectomy? I suppose it was made up by a man since they were profoundly jealous of our ability to carry a fetus. I wondered what precancerous meant. Should I be scared? Was that like being almost pregnant when you knew that was not possible? Precancerous means abnormal cells; I was a member of that club. Ron needed organs to stay alive. I needed organs removed to stay alive. Everyone thought I, too, would die. I didn't think about it. I felt like I was pregnant for the last eighteen months of Ron's life. I was hoping not to feel pregnant anymore.

I had lost much as of late. I wondered where my organs would be without me. I asked my surgeon if I could see my organs after the surgery. He said no. He understood what I didn't. He had lost a son in a snow-and-ice car accident. His son was a junior at West Point.

I was not the oldest person in Roger's class. There was Marilyn Goldstein from Great Neck, Long Island. She was older than me. She was an artist and taught art history, Mayan art, at C.W. Post College in Brookville, Long Island. She had a contagious, loud laugh; she could not contain her emotions. She was funny, honest, and warm. She reminded me of Harvey Fierstein with her large personality. We became friends. I thought everything she wrote was exquisite in its honesty. She was kind and enthusiastic about my words and my work. Marilyn possessed books of knowledge on the Mayans. They were progressive, intuitive warriors. She nurtured us in our artistic endeavors. We were both Jewish widows.

Roger loved to speak. He was witty and chose his words wisely; I did not. I was learning, trying not to use the word "very" since it diminishes what you are saying.

I will never regret attending that conference. He encouraged us to be the best we could. A packet of information was sent to each participant. The last paragraph from Roger stated: "If you are desperate or confused call me. I promise you, your subject is in front of your nose. It could be your nose. See you soon. All the best." He said he wouldn't call us back if our question was "What should I write about?" I never called him, but it was wonderful to know that he cared that much about his students and knew exactly how I felt. He was a special man.

I wanted to thank the powers that be for accepting me into the conference. My plan was to write a mediocre memoir that contained no falsehoods like that nameless Frey guy. The reason for the mediocrity was the lack of falsehoods. The real plan was to write a novella where I could twist the facts willy-nilly. I could be carefree about reality. I wanted to be a sit-down comic and a pre-Alzheimer's chronicler.

The assignment sheet that I received from the conference explained the format we would follow. I hand-delivered the three essays of 1500 words. Roger Rosenblatt suggested we make fifteen copies of each of our essays. We would leave a copy of our work on one pile and pick up a copy of the other workshop participant's work. I managed to forget to collect the other students' work. Marilyn always grabbed two. How did she know I would forget to gather the other student's work? I loved Mayan Marilyn. I have been lucky to find angels who look after me. There was Libby, Marilyn, and Ellen. I know there will be more. Some are real people; some are spirits. I met up with Marilyn later in the day. We ate lunch outside after the essay workshop. She handed me my stack of OPE's, also known as other people's essays. I had homework tonight— cool. Lunch was good with many choices. I was gaining weight. I signed up for a class on being funny. I had to write a short piece; did I say it was supposed to be funny?

Writing funny

I don't do e-mail. My e-mail address is vacationing in southwestern Ibiza. Occasionally, I do Yahoo. I definitely do not Google. Every couple of months, I purchase The Sunday Times. There is so much to read and so little time. I find myself in the Land of Personal Ads, or is it personal abs? Maybe I should hire a personal trainer? I glance at the ads diligently and hopeful but within moments a large wave of nausea comes over me. I have puked on my dream man's ad. Can I find another or is he lost in my last supper? I browse through another ad.

WDMNS [White Divorced Male Nonsmoker] seeks FNS [Female Nonsmoker] who loves Paris, theater, and insects. Pass him by. WSMNS [White Single Male Nonsmoker] seeks friendly WNS [White Nonsmoker] for romantic evenings, cuddling, very slim, and fun-loving. I am not slim anymore and the cuddling is cute, but I am not a hug machine. WDMS [White Divorced Male Smoker] seeks sexy woman to drive with me through the Harley Davidson of life. I like the metaphor. What if he is one large tattoo? What if he wants me to get a tattoo? I don't want to be a biker chick--grow up, take a chance. I listened to his message: "Hi, this is Marty, I live in Brookleen (in Brooklynese). I don't drive a car. I don't have a Harley but if you are interested in walks on the beach, romantic evenings in Prospect Park—call me." I deleted the message and went directly to the Personal Abs section.

I read my funny piece. I was told I lost them at puke. I could change the word. I could leave it as it is, but it's not so funny.

Late one afternoon, I ran into Libby. She was an assistant for Melissa Bank, the author of *The Girls Guide to Hunting and Fishing.* Libby was busy with her own writing, as well as organizing workshops for Melissa.

It was an honor to be an assistant. I think a percentage of the workshop tuition fees are waived. Libby and Melissa became friends. Libby informed me that this evening is the formal dinner outdoors. It was a catered affair. The weather was perfect and I was wearing jeans. Libby suggested I go home immediately to get dressed up.

Shit. I am grateful that I run into people who read the schedule and send me on my way. I had to shower and find a nice dress or long skirt. I leave and speed on home. I showered and put on my long, beige Mexican peasant skirt with a peasant blouse and my dressy straw hat. I drove back to the college clean and ready for dinner. We met in the courtyard of the college. It was serene; everyone was dressed up. I was so grateful that I changed my clothes. The male students were in sport jackets. I am not sure if Billy Collins was or not. There were speeches, laughter, literary innuendo, and double entendre. In other words, it was wonderful. I can't believe I didn't want to go.

It was Thursday so it must be literary essay day. We arrived in class. Roger let us know that we would be writing a piece titled "Last Will and Testament." We all have stories; we all have lives—even those who are eighteen. I remember that I was once eighteen, but I was a young eighteen, whatever that means. I'd have a chance to read my work in front of students who were in Billy Collins's poetry class, Frank McCourt's class, Melissa Banks's novel class, and Marsha Norman's playwriting class. Libby managed not to tell me about this part. I supposed it was in my schedule which I had misplaced or lost. I was at home with my new computer. I needed to write my last will and testament.

I was not sure if we had a time limit on stage to read our work. I was grateful that I was an only child. My piece might be shorter since there were fewer people to leave things to. I left the conference a little early and missed the discussion groups with agents from the publishing houses. I wasn't getting anything published. I wanted to do my assignment.

I refused to call Roger. No one can help me. I was helpless. I struggled. I printed, I deleted, and I wrote some words. I decided it was time for a nap. I couldn't sleep. I went for a walk; I had to pee. I was home and hungry. I made oatmeal for dinner. I liked breakfast food for dinner; granted, some folks would find it bizarre. I think it is bizarre as well. I was finished with my piece three hours later. I read it numerous times so I would be comfortable with it. I printed enough copies for the entire workshop: the professors, students, kitchen staff, gardeners and bartenders. I didn't have to make any copies this time. I might have destroyed a tree or two in the process. I was sorry for my carelessness.

It was my turn to read my piece. Everyone's work so far was good; mine was not. I wore jeans and a black tee shirt. I was not told about the dress code for a reading. The sea of faces was eager to hear each word. I was at the podium with my piece in hand. I was nervous, but the microphone helped me. I adjusted it to my height. Roger was in the first row where my classmates sat, watched, and listened.

My Last Pill and Testament or Who Gets My Stuff

First off, whoever has the most stuff doesn't win. That is why I am going through a shitload of it. I hope to make it easier for you, Adam. To Donald Golden, I leave my signed copy of Allen Ginsberg's Collected Poems 1947-1980. Daniel donated it to the Westhampton Beach Library Sale. I purchased it. Maybe it needs to go back to him or the library.

To Be Nice Bernice, my mother, who predeceased me. I leave thirteen years and one for good luck of unconditional love. Thirteen years of frozen snicker bars, pistachio, and coffee ice cream.

In memory of the thirteen unlucky years, we did not speak to one another.

To Adam Kane, my son, you are outstanding. Diabetes sucks. I think I was more devastated by your illness than you were. I have always believed that some people get the bad stuff out of the way early in life. My wish is that for you.

Call Marvin, our CPA, he will tell you about the money stuff.

To my hospice patient, Louis, who is ninety-three years bold. He greets me cheerily as I visit with him in my Mini Cooper that he calls a Morris. I don't have the heart to tell him it's not a Morris anymore. Sometimes I call it Morris as well. I leave him my "DO NOT RESUSCITATE" bracelet. He will now have one for each wrist or two on one wrist. I also leave him my miniature, Mini Morris Cooper.

To Ron, Ronnie, Ronald, the widow maker. I want to tell you that you taught me by example to stretch myself. I am fifteen pounds heavier. There is a slight chuckle from the audience. *My life is rich and full.*

At this point, my voice is trembling and the paper is shaking. I begin to sneak off the stage. I take tiny ballet steps, as if I would not be noticed. Roger motions to me to get back on stage. I shake my head no. I am about to walk down the steps, but he motions me to continue. I begin to baby ballet step it back to the microphone. I know my voice will crack.

Ron, Ronnie, Ronald, the widow maker. I can never lose you again. That is a blessing. The tears roll down my face, I am nasal. The paper is shaking. *You suffered too much, yet I never realized how hopeful you were through it all. It kind of shocks and amazes me. I thought you were incapable of hope.*

I wanted to crawl off the stage, go home, and remain in the fetal position for a month or two. I was glad that I read my work. I was grateful that Roger encouraged me to complete it. I knew that my walking on and off the stage took time, and my sobbing took time away from others. I was sorry. It was a long day. I left the auditorium for thirty minutes. I returned to the auditorium. I was ready to listen to other readers. Later in the afternoon, a young man read his work, laughing out loud without control. Did I inspire that? Did he feel the need to lighten up the day? I loved it.

I continued to listen to my fellow students. I enjoyed the students' work. I was over my head. I think there was serious talent in my midst. They were young, gifted, and in possession of time to ripen, to perfect their craft. There were more readings. Marsha Norman had her play *Cariboo* performed in the theater. She played softball on Sundays. I didn't partake; I didn't want to be the one last chosen on the team again. It was an exciting, exhausting conference. I will never forget or regret it. Marilyn and I exchanged phone numbers. She lived in Great Neck. I said my goodbyes a day early, no baseball for me.

"I just get home and then I leave again. It's long ago and far away," sings Diana Krall from her song "Departure Bay." The quiet after guests leave was welcoming but no more.

4

MFA STUDENT

Somewhere between here and there, I applied to the Southampton MFA program as a student in search of a degree at fifty-eight years old. They pieced together my transcript from Franklin Pierce College, which is now a university. Back in 1969, I graduated with a major in English and sociology. I suffered through all the other subjects. I assumed my professors suffered more than I did, having witnessed my lack of potential. I lived with the anxiety of being average or below adequate.

I was accepted into the MFA program. I felt proud and nervous. I had someplace to go once a week. I flunked bereavement; I was moving on. As a student in the writer's program, we didn't take tests; we wrote our stories.

Libby recommended that I take Lou Ann Walker's class on the

personal essay. We met on Tuesdays from two to five p.m. We sat in a classroom; our words were analyzed with careful criticism, to the thought and content... Marilyn was my classmate. Bill Weinstein, a friend of Libby's, was in the class. I think he was as old as Marilyn. His wife Karen was a bit younger than me. Libby met them at yoga. It was an honor to be in the class. The students were smart and young with lots of years ahead of them. Life is not perfect because you are young. If you want to be a writer, then chances are you have a boatload of strange family history just begging to be unleashed and shared. Lou Ann was a warm, funny, intellectual woman.

I wasn't sure if it was the combination of Lou Ann and Marilyn but what I wrote in that class I felt good about. People laughed and said I was clever. I had a ball. I became somewhat proficient at writing an essay. It had a beginning, middle, and end. When it was done, I was done with it. No commitment. I waited for the next assignment. I enjoyed the detachment that the essay provided me with. I moved on.

The kids in the class were supportive and kind. I loved their stories about grandma, disabled uncles with unusual talents, cheating fathers, and alcoholic mothers. Some were Adam's age. Adam's gifts were sports and the gift of gab. He could sell you most anything. He couldn't sell me anything. I wasn't buying. Lou Ann had a bag of tricks up her sleeve. Her writing assignments were challenging, always funny, and always fun. Thanks, Lou Ann and in her words:

A Sampling of Lou Ann
Week One: Home
Week Two: The Diatribe
Week Three: The Family Portrait
Week Four: Journal Entry
Week Five: Function over Form

Week Six: Email Essay
Week Seven: Consolation
Week Eight: Epistolary
Week Nine: A Little More Outrage or Outrageousness
Week Ten through Twelve: Your Choice

"We are about to embark upon a rather complex field: The personal essay has no real parameters. An essay can be quite lengthy, or a mere few paragraphs. The essay can be on any subject imaginable: war, peace, obesity, literature, hula hoops, Ouija boards are all topics for an essay or parts of an essay. There is one requirement: Using 'I,' at least once."

Marsha doesn't like e-mail. E-mail pisses me off, but I was forced to have an e-mail address. I might have more than one. In fact, it took two hours to create the address. I decided on using my middle name, Dayvie. It was spelled Davie on my birth certificate. My mother's father's name was David. I should have kept the original spelling, but I changed it in my mind so long ago that I forgot the way it was intended. Be Nice Bernice's middle name was June. Our grandmother's name was May. Be Nice gave herself the middle name June. I considered myself lucky; I could have been named January or February.

In Lou Ann's class I wrote an essay about my cousin:

Ellen, My Virtual Sister

Ellen and I are sisters by cousinhood. We shared our grandmother. However, I thought grandma was all mine since she took up residence in our apartment. In thinking it over again, we, meaning my father and me, became residents in her apartment. I was conceived in my grandmother's apartment.

In the past, I smugly told people that we inherited Grandma; clearly, Grandma inherited us. The truth was I have a miserable time telling schoolmates, teachers, and parents of friends that I had no siblings, even though we called them sisters and brothers back then. I let them know that I indeed had a grandmother.

I guess it was uncommon then to be an only, lonely child. I never really understood. Why? Why was it odd, or were my parents odd? I thought it was a smart idea to mention having a grandmother. It gave our family a sense of normalcy

I was tiny and undernourished like an inhabitant of a third-world country. When I was ten, I looked six. That's how it came to be—they would put other people's new, striking clothes on me, dress me up for display, and snap photos—smile, look surprised.

My cousin, Judy, died shortly after she was married. Her uterus was pregnant with malignant cells, no fetus, just cancer. Now, Ellen and I are utterly uterus less. Ellen was much younger than I when she had the surgery but not nearly as young as Judy.

Yesterday, Ellen called me and left a message: "It's your birthday soon; I saw a great bracelet. Call me back." Ellen is sweeter than I am. She remembers very little about the family. She trusts me to fill her in on the facts. I remember her house as if I occupied the walls. I remember the house far more than she does. This is not important—just the truth.

The house was unlike any I had ever visited. There was a spiral staircase where I often imagined Loretta Young gliding down the steps. The den where Ellen and Judy's father held court housed a bar and the wood flooring was imported from

England. The leather couches, oversized in a coffee or chocolate color, cushioned me beyond comfort.

Their father, Uncle Al, was never without a cigar, cigarette, or cigarillo. My uncle inhaled and exhaled every legal but deadly substance. His tobacco was stored in a humidor. Who knew tobacco required humidity?

Grandma would visit with them on many occasions. She was treated like royalty. I had sleepovers at the house. Judy and I were close in age, though Judy was mature and savvy. She tugged me around like a suitcase she prayed she would never have to open. I was wishing that I could be deposited someplace so I wouldn't make a fool of myself in front of Judy's friends.

Now the years have more importance, if only because the time on the left side represents the time passed and the right is what remains. The thing is, I don't want to celebrate the passage of time with candles, cakes, and presents. I like to celebrate other people's moments.

I was under the impression that Ellen and I had an understanding. We loved to buy gifts; we loved to give gifts. I put a ban on it. It was getting out of control. I read an essay by Adam Gopnik about a very adult-like three-year-old whose imaginary friend Charlie was too busy to be an imaginary friend to her. This was published in The New Yorker, Sept.30th 2002. Charlie was a New York imaginary friend; therefore, the rules are different. I wanted to explain to Ellen the new rules of gift giving, just for us. I would like to initiate an imaginary gift-giving ritual. Ellen said, "What do you mean? What are the rules?" I don't know but I am working on it.

I asked Ellen if she would like an imaginary Porsche for her birthday. No, she says, I want world peace. She is so noble; she was about to take off for New Orleans to assist and organize post-Katrina when she developed bronchitis. I breathed a sigh of relief. I tell Ellen I'll settle for a world that still exists. I'm not as idealistic as her.

How about virtual gift giving? You gift me the world and I will gift you world peace. I don't think she is pleased with this arrangement. I tell her I am not averse to a box of Godiva chocolate every month forever, for real, from you.

Lou Ann encouraged us to send our essays out to be published. We needed to write a query letter.

I wrote one to the editor of the *East Hampton Star*:

Dear Ms. Sansegundo,

I am submitting a 655 word essay about my favorite cousin, Ellen.

I am currently enrolled in the MFA program at Southampton College.

I thank you for your time.

Marsha

I returned to class with my query letter. I did not send it out. The letter was the assignment, most of the class wrote letters. I am convinced mine was the blandest, shortest, and dullest. I had not put any effort into it since I worked on the essay. I didn't understand the value of the query letter. I was writing essays: beginning, middle, and end. I did not have a commitment to it once the piece was completed. I enjoyed the detachment at the finish line. I had much to learn. The query letter determined the fate of your piece. It is the first thing that the editor reads. You must entice and interest the editor or reader at the starting line. If your letter is a sleeper, then they probably will not read your sparkly, clever essay. You, as the student, believed your essay was not up to par. The fact is your query letter might be the problem child.

Lou Ann wanted us to be aware of the time of year we were sending our work out. If the time frame was summer, then you might not want to send a piece out that had to do with Halloween. I think if you were writing about shoes the time of year was a non-issue. If you were writing about snowstorms, perhaps you would not send it out in the dog days of August. If it was about a June wedding, you might not send it out during the November and Thanksgiving time frame. It was a lot to think about, but I knew Lou Ann was correct. I believed it took me longer to write the query letter than the actual essay.

The business of pitching your work was work. The class was three hours. We were asked to write a new query letter. On your mark, get set, go. I re-read my essay, hoping for a sign. Where were my angels? Where was my brain? The fun thing about writing class is you were encouraged to sometimes speak out of turn. It was more like a gathering of friends because you spoke among yourselves. You shared and you learned; oh man, you laughed until it hurt.

We locked Bill, the retired attorney, out of the classroom. I am not sure if it was my idea. He went to the copy machine to make sure all of the students would have his work. I didn't use the copy machine at school since it was more than likely I would do what Bill did. I was a Luddite. I went to Staples to have my work copied. Bill made 900 copies by accident. I wanted to avoid that embarrassment. We permitted Bill back into class. We didn't say a word. We were laughing, wailing. It was fun being an older student. I was catching up on the fun I was supposed to have when I was young. We were getting serious about the task at hand. I think another student mentioned gift-giving practices. A light bulb or thunderbolt went off in my pea brain. You must spell the name of the editor correctly. They will not read it; they will toss it. I understood that. I get upset when people think I am "cia" when I am a "sha." Marsha vs. Marcia.

> *Dear Ms. Sansegundo,*
>
> *It is October; there is a chill in the air. The mailboxes are bursting with bushels of gift-giving catalogs.*
>
> *I am submitting a 655 word essay about chocolate, gift giving, and family.*
>
> *I am currently enrolled in the MFA program at Southampton College.*
>
> *Sincerely,*
> *Marsha*

Most of our letters improved. It was a formula. It worked if you reshaped your brain and thought like a salesman. The hard part is that you were selling your soul, your secrets, and your opinions.

Lou Ann asked us to write a piece about ourselves that no one else knew and then rip it up. I did not rip it up. I saved it. I forgot what I wrote. I re-read it. I wondered if by asking us to discard it she knew we might keep it. Questions and answers I will never know. Was the act of writing it and trashing it a form of freeing us?

CRAYOLA

I loved the smell of a fresh box of crayola crayons. The yellow and green box wooed me beyond color. You had a box of twelve if you were poor like me, ninety if you weren't poor, that is.

I think one year I had forty-eight crayons and that was a fine year for crayons. There were some subtle shades, maybe even some glossy ones—purples, magenta, my all time favorites. I remember watching Be Nice Bernice, my mother, applying red lipstick to her fleshy, thick, perfectly shaped lips as she was leaving the apartment to go shopping at Waldbaums or picking my father up at the Continental Ave. subway station stop in Forest Hills. She shortened his trip home. He would not have to take another train or bus ride. Sometimes if Be Nice was in the mood, she would take me with her. Once we were parked in a spot near the subway, she would get in her serious people watching mode. "Marshie, look at that lady with the two pocketbooks, see that boy chewing four packs of gum." I looked though I never saw what she saw. I noticed the people dressed up—women wearing high heels—men with hats. I looked at people's feet. I was curious about how people walked—inturned or bowlegged. I walked with my feet out like an almost ballet dancer in training.

Be Nice would purse her lips in such a manner that I believed she had restless lip syndrome. By doing that thing with her lips, the lipstick would smooth out with a crisp richness of color texture and seduction. She put the lipstick a bit over her lipline to have her lips appear fuller than they were. She put Vaseline on her eyelashes instead of mascara. That was how it went at Be Nice's beauty academy. I was too young for lipstick, too shy for boys and too flat for them to notice me anyway.

I put two of my red jack balls in the bra that I begged Be Nice to buy me. It was basically a bandage with straps with two red jack balls stuffed in to resemble breasts. The things we do to be grown up for the opposite sex. No one noticed me or my jack ball tits.

One morning at Public School 119 where I was bussed in, since the population in Glendale, Queens on the Brooklyn border was decreasing. The principal of the elementary school was Dr. Molloy. She was about 6 feet 2 inches with her old lady shoes with laces. You heard her before you saw her and you never wanted to see her. She had a long horsey face with at least six chins. She was eighty years old. She stood straight with thining red-dyed hair rimless glasses like my grandmother. You somehow knew she went to parochial school where she received catechisms in place of orgasms. She wore wool tweedy skirts with white starched blouses with a single strand of pearls on her thirteen chins. She was stern and didn't like me and my kind. We were the kids that prevented the school from shutting down. The kids from the co-op were from the lower east side, Brooklyn and Queens. We were Jewish, Italian and poor. Glendale had a large German and Scandavian population. I liked the idea that I was being bussed in to another school. Bussing was a political issue back then. African American kids were being bussed into all white schools. It was a good concept that created fear in the parents about children sitting side by side with African American kids. I felt a sadness and connection to that history.

Today was the day that my crayons spoke to me in a way that they should not have. I glanced at the purple crayon. It was a dark rich royal purple. I removed it from its box of twelve.

Eleven crayons remained. Did they miss their royal companion? I took the crayon and put it in my pocket. I raised my hand and asked for the bathroom pass; it was granted to me. I entered the girls room with purple crayon in hand, I approached the mirror, and with my left hand I applied the purple crayon to my naturally dark and thin lips. I now have purple lips and the waxy odor was perplexing me. There was no perfumy odor like real lipstick. My lips are purple and I am in the fifth grade. I look at me and my lips in the mirror; I did not look any more attractive. I feel like I did something right when I know I did something wrong. My little crayon day was really just beginning.

I return to my classroom, Miss Ludwig immediately noticed me and my stupid purple lips. She sends Ingrid to fetch Dr. Molloy for my indiscretion, stupidity or both. I hear her shoes —slow, deliberate steps. The classroom door was open and I know my fate will soon be cast. Dr Molloy walks into the classroom; she asks me to go to her office. She is a mountain at my side. I am the second shortest in the class, Ingrid is even smaller than me. I am an ant at her side and I wish she would just step on me and put me out of my misery. We walk into her office, dark wood furniture formal and frightening. She looks down at me and says, "Does your mother know you are wearing lipstick?" I say, "No this is not lipstick, it is a crayon that I put on my ..." "Young lady, I don't care what color it is, you are not to wear lipstick to school. Do you hear me?" "Yes, but I just wanted to taste the crayon to see if it was like the stuff that my mother puts on her lips" Dr Molloy decides it is time to call home. There are no cell phones, pagers, blueberries, just a black rotary phone. My mother, Be Nice Bernice, was

66

working. Grandma was living with us. Dr Molloy, or her secretary that she was living with, called my house and spoke to my grandmother. Dr Molloy returned to tell me that my grandmother was coming to the school to take me home.

Crazy crocodile tears were rolling down my cheeks and the salty tears sustained me. It was strangely comforting. Bernice, my mother, said I cried crocodile tears. How can you cry crocodile tears? Crocodiles cannot cry. I told Dr Molloy my mother was working and my grandmother did not know where the school was. She said that a neighbor would be bringing her here. I was to be suspended for wearing crayons on my lips. I am sitting in the hall outside of Dr Molloy's office on a chair facing the wall so no one can see my colored lips and I cannot see anyone not looking at me or my lips.

It seemed like forever but Grandma finally arrived. She is wearing a dress. She must have been cooking because I see an apron under her overcoat. We are a pair, Grandma and I; she is not wearing any lipstick and I have my purple passion crayola lips. She never asked a neighbor she just took herself and her apron and called a cab. I kept looking at the apron and wondered if the other kids noticed her attire or if it was only me who noticed.

I wondered why she didn't yell at me, reprimand me or ask what it was I was thinking. I suppose she knew what would happen when I was back home.

We worked in groups. Lou Ann named us the 3 M's: Marilyn, Margaret, and Marsha. Margaret was also a widow. She was younger and a nurse. She met a psychologist at the hospital where she worked. They married; he was married once before. He was older than her. This was her first marriage; she didn't have children. Marilyn had two adopted sons.

One of the exercises we participated in was to define new expressions or new words from our ever-changing vocabulary. We did not have to be accurate. I think we were trying to be humorous.

> *What is a metrosexual?*
>   *1. Someone who uses alternative transportation.*
>   *2. People who have sex on trains in the city.*
>   *3. Someone who engages in sex only in large cities.*

There was more of Lou Ann's bag of writer tricks with a twist. Lou Ann supplied us with questions and we answered them as we wished. These were my responses:

> *If you were stuck in an elevator what would you do?* Pray that I don't pee and pop half of a Xanax.
>
> *If you were stuck in an elevator who would you want to be with?* Al Roker and Ruth Westheimer. They are the luckiest, semi-precious celebrities. I would swallow one whole Xanax and listen to them converse.
>
> *What part of yourself do you conceal?* My three stomachs and bulging midriff.
>
> *Which of your parent's traits did you inherit?* Only the very best, considering the inbreeding.
>
> *What is your favorite inclement weather?* Fog, of course.

What is your least favorite sport? Baseball, too much spitting and scratching.

What is your favorite sport? Watching men spit and scratch.

What is the dumbest thing you ever did? I was performing in a play in college. I was Fifi, the maid. The other actor who was the lead managed to bypass one of my major scenes. I called the suicide hotline as a quasi-prank. The call was traced. I was arrested.

If you could be anyone for one day who would it be? President Bush so I could impeach myself.

If you could be anyone for two days who would it be? Gloria Steinem.

What event would be impossible to attend? The inauguration of another Republican.

If you were stuck in an elevator who would you not want to be with? Tom Cruise.

If you were a tree never mind if you were an insect. What insect would you be? A butterfly, I dream of Nabokov capturing me.

What was the meanest thing you ever did? My husband was about to have the last surgery of his life. We did the gurney kiss waltz dance about a dozen times. This time, I said, "Let's get divorced." I, of course, was joking. He was comatose after the surgery.

Do you have regrets? I regret everything. I regret nothing. Life is regrettable.

If you met the man of your dreams what would you do? I have met him. He is my ex-gardener. I do my best to keep him in my dreams.. Thank you for asking.

I appreciate your honesty. Ta Ta

The semester was winding down. The leaves were changing colors, and the Westhampton wind was stirring. Margaret and I volunteered to buy a present for Lou Ann. Everyone had an opinion, a different one. Someone thought we should buy her jewelry. I was thinking that was too personal. I wanted to get her a gift certificate to a local store. Some students thought it was too impersonal. I gave up on volunteering; I don't recall what we gave Lou Ann as a gift. I enjoyed the time spent with her. She wrote a book, *A Loss of Words*. Lou Ann's parents were mute.

My guide, Libby, suggested Kaylie Jones's class on the novel. Winter was around the corner. I was planning on leaving Westhampton for the winter. I might take Kaylie next September. If I continued to take one class every fall, I would have my MFA as I entered assisted living. However, the summer workshop got me a quick two credits. I enrolled to improve my skills. I was a student hoping to find what I lost. I had to be something. I wanted to learn how to critique others' work.

I suppose I had graduated from essay to novel. I thought the short story would have been wiser. I needed baby steps. The young guided the old. I didn't feel old or young. I felt short.

Kaylie Jones's class met once a week on Tuesday evenings from six to nine p.m. Kaylie lived in the city. She was an attractive blond. She had an eight-year-old daughter. She brought her poodle to class on numerous occasions. I was grateful for the diversion. Her father was James Jones, who wrote *From Here to Eternity*. I wondered if I should read it or watch the movie.

I read *The Age of Innocence* in my innocence. I saw the movie. Winona

Rider was lovely in the Victorian clothes. They were impractical, but the less you show, the more desired you were—maybe? We were required to write a two-page synopsis of the books. My synopsis was two paragraphs. I was tempted to purchase a dog. If I brought my imaginary dog to class and Kaylie brought her dog perhaps there would be numerous distractions, and she won't notice that my synopsis was shrinking in size with each book. Perhaps she won't notice that I was in the class.

Kaylie had us write a list of the books that influenced us.

Stones from the River, by Ursula Hegi tells about people living in a river town in Germany. Trudi the main character is a dwarf. She wants to be normal. Her mother descends into madness. Her father ran a lending library in their home. Her best friend Georg's parents pretend he is a girl and dresses him in dresses. They are both outsiders. The Nazi's would have found them unfit. They would have been cast away. Trudi wants to be normal but discovers that everyone is different. No one is normal. During the war, Trudi hid Jews in her cellar.

> *One True Thing* Anna Quindlan
> *Sophie's Choice* William Styron
> *Alias Grace* Margaret Atwood
> *Night Falls Fast* Kay Redfield Jamison
> *The Liar's Club* Mary Karr
> *The Shipping News* Annie Proulux
> *The Year of Magical Thinking* Joan Didion
> *Eden Close* Anita Shreve
> *Anthropologist on Mars* Oliver Sacks
> *The Reader* Bernard Schlink

On My To Read List:

> *All past, present, and future books by* Kaylie Jones

Kaylie was intellectual and worldly. She grew up in Paris, speaking French and Russian. Her daughter was in gifted classes. I was not alone in concerns over the volumes of reading that were required. Some young students were vocal about the volume and length of the novels.

In The Age of Ignorance by Edith Wharton Newland, Archer loved Countess Olenska not only because of her beauty. She was everything that he was not. He was an Archer. He lived a financially and privileged life. I was not surprised that he wasn't brave enough to visit with Countess Olenska. He asked her how she was able to behave as she does. She was a brave woman. He was not brave. He continued to live his life of quiet desperation. Henry David Thoreau.

My critique of the book was reviewed by a class member who suggested I get the title correct. I thought I did.

Our first assignment was to write a synopsis of our novel. I had many ideas but I was not sure which one to tell. They blended in ways that they shouldn't. There were broken dreams, lost time, illnesses inherited, and disinherited people. I needed new ways to pass time to find the earth under my feet stable and forgiving.

My book was about a woman who marries a man her mother loved before she did, though not in the biblical sense. Nola met Mark at a club in 1969. She was young, but she wasn't stupid. She never knew how to please her demanding, erratic, seductive, glamorous, tomboy parent. Nola married Mark and Be Nice Bernice, her mother, was temporarily and sporadically happy. Nola loved Mark, though he was not her love lust. They had an exceptionally beautiful child after a miscarriage.

Mark had numerous illnesses. They were complicated and serious. There was the long-awaited kidney transplant, the uninvited stroke, and then the paralysis, confusion, and death. Nola finds strength in Mark's *courage*. Perhaps there was a reason why the word "rage" resides in the word courage.

Kaylie read our synopsis, she advised us on the path she saw our books taking. She told me my book was about a mother who has an affair with her daughter's boyfriend. I was befuddled and paralyzed; my story seemed foreign to me from the beginning. It remained that way for the duration of the class.

I created my own curriculum. We were asked to write a book report on the novels we read. Instead of continuing with Kaylie's instructions on my novel and Be Nice's alleged affair with my boyfriend, I did a Woody Allen-type thing where my character or I was incorporated in the book report. Kaylie, though younger, became my mother. I could never please Kaylie in my writing so I took another path.

Once Nola was back in the house that she and Mark built from scratch, Mark died in the house where she would do her best not to die in. This was the same house in which she picked up some cute guy. She had adequate sex in the king-sized bed, as well as the queen-sized bed.

He called her a complacent pragmatist and she wished him an indifferent Thanksgiving. Other than that they had little to say to one another.

She had homework to do. She was attending classes at the local university. Nola knew she would not finish her degree in time, the question being in time for what. Nola thought it would be a hoot if, the day of her funeral, she could receive her degree posthumously so it would save her guests one extra trip.

Nola needed to read Mating by Norman Rush. It was about an agricultural anthropologist. Did you know that when anthropologists get together, they talked about food? Mating was 477 pages.

According to Norman Rush, "There must be such a thing as situational madness, because I was on the verge of it. I know that schizophrenics hear people murmuring when the bed sheets rustle or when the vacuum cleaner is on."

Nola was on the verge of ripping the book to shreds. She did not need the sound of the vacuum cleaner to put her in a state of situational madness. Thank you, Norman Rush.

The semester was coming to an end. I missed numerous classes since I was behind in my writing and well behind in the reading assignments—very behind.

I purchased the book *Poetics of Space* by Gaston Bachelard: "The classic look at how we experience intimate spaces." I was not able to understand much in the book. I didn't have the requisite patience to read it. I shunned it; I put it aside. I knew where it lived in my house, but I avoided it intentionally. I had a friend who travels with this book and has read it in its entirety many times. It is a treasured book to her.

There is a book called *Comfortable with Uncertainty: 108 Teachings on Cultivating Fearlessness and Compassion* by Pema Chodron, an American Buddhist nun. I have never read this book. I travel with it, if only for the cover picture. It is a black-and-white photo of the wildness of the ocean. A person in shorts and a tee shirt contemplates the water. There is a wood deck with steps that provide access and protection from the waves. The water is churning wild with strong winds. I cannot see the sky. Did someone take this photo in the midst of a hurricane? The book does not give credits for the photo. It is a mystery.

On the day of my last class with Kaylie Jones which was not the last day of the semester, I gave Kaylie *Poetics of Space.* I don't know why. She surely must have the book. I knew I didn't want the book in my possession anymore. I hoped that one day I would read the book but not today. I wasn't sure I had a story to tell. It certainly was hiding from me. It was living somewhere in me that I was not able to reach. It grew further away from me. We avoided each other: me and my story. We lost contact. We rarely thought in story form. It was no longer a story. It was my life.

The weather was shifting and my heart was cold. The Hamptons was a resort and, after Thanksgiving, the herds thinned out. The deer go into the rut and I do too. My rut differs from the mating rituals of deer. I felt sleep deprived, even after a full eight-hour rest. I felt ancient, lonely, and cold. I use to enjoy the changing of the seasons, I was part of the change. I think I was part of the problem. I will miss the time spent with the students, Kaylie and her dog. I had a place to go. It took about thirty minutes or so to drive to class. It was time to move on. The drowsy, hibernating polar bear that was me, without Ron, had surfaced.

5

TANGO FRACTURES

As a child, we moved every three years. We moved to a different apartment; my father always striving for better. My mother was a willing participant. She would announce that it was an arduous task to remove everything from the walls and return them to their habitats, after the painters had painted. In one not-so-quick swoop, she would have the apartment boxed up, never to replace an item on that wall. No paint, just a new place. If I wasn't careful, I might be boxed up and hauled onto the moving truck.

We actually lived near every neighborhood on the Queens Independent Subway Line. We lived in Long Island City, Jackson Heights, Rego Park, Forest Hills, and Jamaica Estates. The apartment in Long Island City was a housing project—a brand new apartment for us.

I remembered our rental experience years later. It was when we were having the house built in Westhampton. We sold the split level type house in Lawrence, New York, near JFK International Airport. We rented a three-bedroom, summery cottage near the country club in Westhampton Beach that did not allow Jews as members. We rented it for $800 a month from September to May in the off season. The owners lived in Rye, New York. The house did not have air conditioning, but every room had a ceiling fan. It was furnished with dainty Victorian style furniture and fabrics. I was fine with it. Ron was not. It was dainty, and it didn't suit him. I explained that was the art of renting; you don't care because it was a short stay. Perhaps short stays didn't mean the same thing to me as Ron. He might have known his life and health were compromised. His time on the planet shortened. He certainly liked the price. It was a bargain. The house we were building would take a year to complete. We were dependent on the type of winter we would have. We knew we would need another furnished rental. The season began on Memorial Day weekend.

I was trained to be nomadic by my parents, but my parents weren't nomadic. They were impulsive, especially my father. He was restless. I was nomadic in reverse. I left home for periods of time to discover vestiges of myself by living elsewhere. There was a difference.

I was empty and spent, but there was gas in my Mini Cooper.

I went to a beauty salon in town. My hair goes from gray to brown in under two hours. The hairdresser was also a realtor. Joyce the realtor/hairdresser told me about a house we could rent by the week. It was furnished with three bedrooms. It had air conditioning, and we could wait comfortably for our house to be completed. Most of the time, life is a waiting game. Sometimes, we wait and the game is lost. The surviving children were having a difficult time—making a decision on what to do with the house. Joyce suggested they rent it to us until they decided. The house was old and in need of a paint job. It would be a short stay. This was the second house we rented since the house we were building was turning into a full-term pregnancy, with heartburn, headaches, and weight gain in the process. I knew a smoker had lived in it—the stale, stagnant smell of nicotine. I wondered how a smoker and non-smoker could live together, make love, and not be repulsed by the other and the odor. I suppose sex was about longing, love, need, and odors. I smoked; Ron never did. We would wait with anticipation and joy for the birth of the house.

While Ron was watching CNN or Geraldo Riviera, I rummaged through boxes filled with photos of the family whose home we lived in. I filtered through cards, official documents, death certificates, and birth certificates. The Quinns had four children: three girls and one boy. I looked through drawers and cabinets as if I was the surviving child. I did what they could not.

"A cabinet opened is a world revealed, drawers are places of secrets, and with every habitual action we open endless dimensions of our existence." *The Poetics of Space* by Gaston Bachelard

My snooping ways taught me that we all suffer. The paintings on the walls of the house were works by the mother and one of the daughters. While Ron was at his treatments, I was obsessed with the family. I created a timeline of their lives. The mother was one of the first women in the Coast Guard. She was an artist and teacher. I thought about them while I lived in their house; I thought about them when we moved into our new house.

BACK ON THE ROAD

I rented an apartment in Boca Raton, Florida, for three months from January through March. I was emailed photos of the apartment since I had never seen it in person. It was a compact, two- bedroom apartment near Mizner Park. It was not too far from the ocean. It was another brand-new apartment for me since I didn't have Ron to keep me warm. My goose down comforters did a fine job but they were hardly good enough.

It was 1,323 miles to Boca Raton, Florida, a twenty-two hour road trip. I lived on the eastern tip of Long Island. I knew people who did the trip in two days, but there were usually two of them. They took turns sleeping and driving. Me and Me Inc. started early and looked for a motel about an hour before dusk.

I left on Christmas Day. Most people were where they needed to be. My lease began on January 1. I planned to visit with Ellen and stay over one night with her, Jamey, and Max the dog. They lived in Perry Point, Maryland, in a haunted mansion. Ellen declared that they were friendly ghosts. I slept there on a number of occasions, and I heard a lot of pipes banging. Was it the plumbing? Was it the friendly ghosts? Jamey worked for the Veterans Administration as the head of the South Eastern Region. They lived in a government-owned home near Havre de Grace, with stunning water views in the middle of nowhere. This was my longest road trip. I hoped I would stay awake—stay alive. I was grateful that I was able to leave Dodge when the weather changed. The truth is that the weather gets dreary in November. I was born in November; I was almost born on Halloween. The many hours in the car will be offset by three months of Florida sunshine and light. I will be a snowbird. I will outsmart winter.

The drive was always tedious but in the tedium I planned what to do next. I saw the Broadway show *Forever Tango*. I was in love with everything *tango*, from the stiletto heels to the black revealing dresses, to the men who move and the women who let the men lead in the dance of life and sex. It has been said that the intensity of the tango is such "that you are never sure if they will have sex or kill each other." From the playbill of the show *Forever Tango.*

The apartment was cozy and modern. I unpacked my clothes. There were dishes since it was fully equipped with all that I needed. I brought my own towels and sheets, not that I needed to.

I was overly concerned about falling on ice, as well as shoveling my driveway and car. The winter was painful without Ron. He was my sunlight even in his darkest depression and despair. He was there. I lost myself in taking care of him.

The following day, I had dinner at an Italian restaurant, thinking that tomorrow I will join a gym. Out of the corner of my eye, I spied a magazine about Boca Raton. I picked it up. I went back to the apartment. I leafed through the magazine, and there was a new LA Fitness not too far from my apartment. I decided to join. I noticed an advertisement for tango lessons. I was in the right place.

I called the gym and the dance studio. The following day I was a member of LA Fitness. Friday night featured a complimentary tango lesson for beginners. Count me in! I found the local library. I needed to be near books. I took a ride to the ocean. It was an hour before dusk. I walked on the beach. The color of the sky turned the color of pinkish orange and blue ice. The water was green, rough, and the sand felt light on my toes. This was my personal pedicure.

I was not sure if I would go to the gym or to the tango lessons. I liked the idea that the gym was brand new. It was Friday night. I decided it would be Tango Friday for me.

The plan was to dance myself out of widow land by studying and learning the tango. On my fifth day in Boca, in 2/4 time, I was down for the count. I didn't take one graceful or clumsy move. I never made it to the tango class. I flopped on a stone floor in a restaurant around the corner from the tango studio.

I was ambulanced to the Boca Raton Community Hospital. The

ambulance ride was a virgin one for me. I had been in countless ambulances but never in a reclining position. The light in the ambulance disturbed my eyes. I covered my face in an ostrich-like fashion. The vehicle made tangoesque turns. A pregnant woman could miscarry or deliver on one of those swift maneuvers.

"What happened to you in the restaurant?" It is a voice, not the one in my head that begs to forget where I am. Can I answer without removing the blanket from my head? I fell as I was leaving the restaurant. I lowered the blanket to my chin. I closed my eyes. The light was harsh. I think my elbow's dangling—disconnected from the joint.

The man examines my arm with caution. "You might have dislocated your shoulder. How's the pain?" I don't feel pain. I re-covered my eyes with the blanket and waited.

I was wheeled out of the ambulance into the hospital. There was some kind of traffic jam in the corridor, a delay. I was not an emergency. I will be patient. I was in no hurry to discover what I had done.

I was at the mercy of Dr. Do Good. I was situated in a room; a gentlemen with a pad walks in. I was jealous of anybody who was mobile. I was greedy; I wanted to tango, to dance.

"How do you spell your name?"

"Which one?"

"Both names." I gave him my wallet. I asked if he would remove my insurance card for me. My left arm was fine. The man with the pad found my insurance card; that's all he wanted anyway. I was examined, x-rayed, and questioned. A doctor was in possession of my file, ergo I existed. My jeans needed to be cut off in order for me to be examined and x-rayed. I was curious and anxious about how I was going to return to my apartment without my clothes. The jeans that were cut off were my favorite ones.

"I'm Dr. Sutter. I have read your x-rays. Your elbow was fractured at the point." I also needed surgery on my left knee in half an hour.

"Doctor, what was wrong with my knee?"

"You have lacerations in your knee; we need to stitch it up for you."

I needed fifteen stitches. With my one functional limb, I lifted my blanket over my head and waited. My phone was ringing; it could be hiding anywhere. I was in no condition to play hide and seek with my phone. I buzzed for the nurse. I know they don't always come in emergencies, but I was not an emergency, just an emerging fool who wanted her phone and wanted to learn how to dance the tango.

Dr. Sutter returned as he promised. He found my phone and I noticed Adam had called. With my very perfect, single limb, I dialed Adam.

"Hi, Mom, I thought you would be in the apartment."

"Yeah, I thought so too." Dr. Sutter was numbing my knee. Adam asked where I was.

"I fell. I'm in the hospital."

"Very funny, Mom."

"I'm serious." I told him I was fine, not really fine, but I would be. "Please don't worry and don't tell Grandpa… I love you."

Dr. Sutter operated on my left knee. I had never fallen before. I was stitched up. I hoped they could stitch up my jeans the way they stitched my knee. My right elbow was in a sling; I was told that I needed surgery on my elbow. I was going home shortly. I was returning to the Boca apartment by cab without my DKNY jeans.

A hospital gown was my attire for the cab ride home. I brought blankets from the bed to be worn as a cover-up. I looked like a homeless person or an escapee from a psychiatric ward. The cab driver dropped me off with my new friends: a cane and a pair of crutches. I used whatever was more comfortable for me. The cab driver pretended I was not there. He asked for the fare. I paid him and asked if he would open the cab door for me. He sat there waiting for me to get out of his cab. I opened the cab door with my left hand, left the door open, and walked off.

The cab driver had to get out of his cab to close the damn door. I managed to put my two feet on the ground, gather my blankets, and find the buzzer to let myself into the lobby. I hobbled to the elevator. I was safely in my apartment. My eighty-five years old, widowed father, who lived in Ft. Lauderdale, called me on my cell to let me know that he spoke to Adam. He wanted to help me. He was forty minutes away and wanted to see me. I gave him the address. I told him he didn't have to come. He insisted. I felt heavy and awkward. I was a polar bear without beautiful white fur. I was sluggish and numb. I didn't feel pain. I was bandaged. I was wounded. I was alive. My father knocked on the door. He drove in the rain to help me. We were widowed within months of each other.

He looked at the damage I did to my limbs and told me what a lovely apartment I was renting. He had a girlfriend and gave me the ginger ale he had in the trunk of his car for her. I was grateful. I thanked him. He asked what I needed him to do, and I told him I was glad he had come. I was sleepy. I told him to go home.

I managed to find my bed and a can of ginger ale by my side. I was not taking my pills tonight. They gave me a prescription for painkillers. Painkillers made me nauseous, and I was not going to be nauseous today.

I was not experiencing any physical pain. My adrenaline was protecting me. I began to sob. My tears streamed down my cheeks. I glanced in the mirror only to discover that my cheek bones had purple-yellow bruises that looked like salami and eggs but not good enough to eat. I was nasally, sniffling, and cold. I felt stupid. I had the good fortune of being able to escape the winter to try to enjoy what was left of my life, and I blew it. How stupid of me to think I could learn the tango? How foolish of me to make plans. I couldn't write the book Kaylie advised me to write. I couldn't write the book I wanted to write. I wanted to leave New York. I wanted to dance. I wanted to be free.

If I had the energy I would laugh, but the tears were easier… It felt right as rain. I cried myself a small river and fell asleep.

One year after Be Nice died, my father met a woman. He was eighty-two and she was seventy-two. I wondered how it was so easy for my father to meet someone. My father would ask me how I could remain single after Ron's death. I gave it some thought. I never knew why it wasn't important to have a man in my life. I needed to take care of myself. I wanted to take care of myself. I was fearful of having to be a caregiver again. I was glad that my father met someone. In reality, it made it easier for me. If he had someone in his life, he would be busy with her. He took terrific care of my mother. He deserved happiness. I was seeking happiness on a different path. I wanted to be able create happiness within myself. I was nomadic and social. I made friends and enjoyed friendships but I could say no. I could say yes. I could choose, be free to be me. I wondered if a part of me was jealous of how easy he could find another. I felt that a man in my life was not part of the equation. When my father asked why I did not find a replacement for Ron, I felt inadequate.

I learned that there were more women than men, and any man over a certain age that could drive was a commodity. My father was a commodity. He drove; he looked fifteen years younger than his eighty-two years. The single women in his community would leave casseroles outside his door.

When I awoke the next morning, I was uncomfortable. I had to call my insurance company. My HMO was better known as Horrible Medical Options Inc. My call was important to them. I was napping intermittingly; twenty minutes flew by. I was of no importance but my call was important. I had to listen to terrible music until someone answered the phone. I had my cell phone in my ear. I was bored and impatient. I was a patient without a doctor. A live voice on the other end of the line asked me for my personal information. I was humbled beyond obscurity. The person on the phone requested information, facts that I know she was in possession of. This was for my protection in case someone desired to steal my life. I was wondering exactly who that might be.

I was ready to go forward with the surgery on my elbow. The insurance company representative informed me that my coverage only covered me if I was in New York. If there was an emergency, then they would treat it. The surgery on my knee was an emergency because of the bleeding. The elbow, I was told, was not an emergency, and I needed to go back to New York to have the surgery there. I asked to speak to a supervisor. I listened to more crummy music. I'd rather hear nothing than elevator music. There should be a button that I could press to rid my ears of this music, but there was not. A person claiming to be a supervisor told me the same thing. I told them that I was in no position to travel and I will have the surgery in Florida. I told them I will send in an appeal. I asked them to send me the paperwork and I would worry about it later.

I called the woman that I rented the apartment from. I asked her if she knew of an orthopedist, and she gave me the name of a doctor. I made an appointment. I spoke to my father and told him that I would need surgery on my elbow. I told him I would take a cab to the outpatient facility on the day of the surgery. I asked him if he would pick me up after the surgery. He was okay with that. I thanked him for taking the time.

The visit to the orthopedist went well. He told me that I broke the elbow at the point. I asked him why it was called a funny bone. There wasn't much funny going on with my bone. The surgery was scheduled. I gave my father the address of where I was having the surgery. I remembered seeing him as I was wheeled to where he was sitting. He looked fit and healthy for an old guy. I was in a wheelchair and my elderly father was helping me.

I hadn't eaten for a while. My father suggested PF Chang's. I was not sure what they injected me with for the surgery, but I was flying. I was talking nonstop. My father told me he didn't know I was funny. I realized he didn't know me at all. I was glad that he was there. He drove me back to my apartment. I thanked him and told him I would be fine and then he drove back home.

The surgery went well. It was an olecranon fracture. I was repaired; there were pins and wires in my right elbow.

I wasn't able to bathe myself. I couldn't drive. In fact, my car was still parked near the restaurant which was next door to the tango studio. The owner of the restaurant called and volunteered to deliver the car back to me. He came to my apartment and I gave him the key to my car. I thought that was nice of him, and I waited for the day that I would be able to drive it myself.

I was within walking distance to a bagel place, a video store, and a pizza parlor. I hired Ndaye from Haiti to help me bathe and buy groceries. She came for three hours, three times a week. I had all that I needed.

A shower was tricky so she gave me a sponge bath and washed my hair. We went out to lunch. She was a nice young woman. We were walking distance to some antique shops and she had an eye for pretty things.

The weather was lovely. Ndaye helped me for two weeks and then I thought it was time to go it alone. I was in a deep sleep. I heard what sounded like a fire alarm. Oh shit, was there a fire? Was I dreaming? I woke quickly. I was not dreaming. I grabbed my bright-orange, iridescent rain slicker, my crutches, my pocketbook, my keys, and my wallet. My right arm was in a sling. I looked like a Halloween pumpkin in the wrong season. I locked the apartment door. The elevators were not functioning. I was living on the sixth floor and I would be walking down double flights with my slicker and crutches. I walked slowly. I couldn't afford another fall. I didn't know what time it was. I was outside the building where the residents gathered. It was two-thirty a.m. I heard people talking; they have been told it was a fire drill. I overheard that new buildings have to practice for the real fire. I should have brought my cell phone in case I had another emergency but I think like a person on crutches.

Do we have to trek back upstairs or will the elevators be working? I knew where my car was. I could sleep in it. I followed the crowd back to the building. We walked up the steps to sleep, and I thought if there was another fire drill that I would go back home to winter.

Two weeks after the first drill, I awoke to another alarm. Was I imaging the sound? It was the alarm. Should I get up and go down the steps? Maybe this was a fire. I didn't smell smoke. This time I wrapped a long shawl around me. I realized that was not a great idea; I might trip on the shawl. I did the walk down the steps; this time I was walking better. I was outdoors; the fire drill party ended early, no fatalities. It was time to walk up the stairs back to my apartment if it happens again, I will take some medication and sleep like a baby. I might take a pill tonight.

Two weeks after the surgery on my elbow, the stitches were removed and a cast was put on. I began physical therapy, three days a week. The stitches on my knee had been removed. I was being fixed. The physical therapy was an hour for each session. I basically had to strengthen my elbow and fingers since they were residing in a cast. It was slow but I was not in pain. They prescribed OxyCodone, OxyContin, Tramadol, and a few oxymorons in the evening with diet soda. I filled the prescriptions and hoarded them in case I needed to make a quick, quiet exit from the planet. I realized I could keep them beyond their expiration date if they were in fact going to be used as an exit. I never swallowed any of the pain pills. I did my therapy. I never missed a session. I wanted to be put back together, unlike Humpty Dumpty.

I would take a cab to therapy. After therapy, there was a mall where I would walk and browse the shops. I would take me and the pins in my elbow for a stroll. I went out to lunch or dinner. I found a library and a second-hand bookshop. I went to Barnes and Noble and read parts of many books.

One day, I called the cab company to take me to therapy. He arrived late. As I was getting out of the cab, I was carrying some of the equipment that I used at home for exercising. I wasn't able to open the door of the cab.

I asked the driver if he could open the door for me.

"No lady, I can't." I realized he was overweight but with my elbow not up to par, I struggled and he watched. I slammed the door shut with my foot. I was thinking of going home and trying the pain pill Tramadol. I didn't, but I was mad as hell.

I called the cab company and asked for a driver for an earlier time so I would not be late. I waited for what seemed like forty-five minutes. I was ready TO WALK TO THERAPY. I went to the garage and drove my car to physical therapy.

I did my exercises twice a day. I was getting better. A friend of mine was planning on visiting me. She booked a flight but when I told her about my fracture; she cancelled the trip. She wanted to visit with me only if I was feeling good enough to entertain her. I understood, I don't think that is the kind of friend I am or aspire to be.

6

WRITING WORKSHOP IN
BOCA RATON

❦

I went to the Mizner Park area near the library where there was a community center for seniors. Among the class brochures, I found a memoir-writing class for seniors. I was a senior; I thought I might have extra time in my pocket. The memoir class met on Wednesdays from one to three-thirty p.m. I signed up for the class.

I felt like an addict looking for an AA group. My addiction was storytelling. My drug was words; my passion was sentences. It was not dangerous. My joy was evoking emotion in others: laughter or tears. I was not particular as long as I had a pad and a pen—I would be fine. The members of the class were older. They literally had war stories to tell. It was less formal than the MFA classes. We wrote, we read, and we brought one copy of our piece for the teacher. The class listened and some students or members commented on our work. We sat at a rectangular table. The classes were inexpensive, and some people didn't show up every week, but I was a regular.

A writing group is made up of folks who love and respect the written word. The written word is concrete. It is opaque. We are readers and writers. We were born to tell our stories.

There was something to be said about tables: circular, rectangle, or oblong. You had your place. There was someone on your left and right. You shared a piece of yourself, but kept parts in reserve.

Emily Rosen, the teacher, was a writer for the local newspaper. At the first class she had a bag of things for us to write about. She had a hairbrush, Radio Shack battery, pretzels, tin foil, and a can of soda in her bag.

Our life was waiting to become a memory. Once again, I found my voice in the written word: "Sticks and stones may break my bones, but words will never hurt me."

I wrote the following piece:

> The written word stands alone, it can shine from above.
> It can pull you in and twist you about.
> It can make you frown, laugh, or shriek in terror
> You may cry, you may lie. You will walk away with a thought.
> You may know the reason you lied. For the lie will tell the truth.
> You will lose the lie. You will lose it in the trash of ancient pain.
> You learn to trust your lies. They reveal what you need, when you are ready.

I wrote about Radio Shack. I wrote about how clever I thought they were to have survived in business for decades. After class, I drove to a local restaurant. I was becoming a true Floridian.

I had an early dinner. I drove to T.J. Maxx. I felt the need for some retail therapy. I looked around the store. It felt superb to be out and about doing regular, stupid things. I purchased a pair of jeans similar to the ones that were cut off me at the scene of the crime. They fit well.

I purchased blouses and shoes: flats, no more heels for me.

I looked forward to the writing class. I didn't have the trepidations that I had at the conference or Kaylie's class. I was passing time in the company of other writers. I liked the fact that I found the class by accident. I knew there were no accidents.

I was a good healer; I did my therapy. I thought about what to write. It was the day of the class. I had nothing to say. I had no ideas. I was luckier than most; I had angels that led the way. Emily Rosen asked if she could include this.

Ellen arrived from Maryland as Ron took his last breath. She's good at making arrangements.

The night nurse who was taking care of Ron in the house said that she would be leaving as Ron, too, was leaving us. The hospice nurse arrived, took his pulse that he did not have, and checked his heart. She then poured the morphine down the kitchen sink.

I wanted to know what morphine tasted like and why Ron grimaced when I gave it to him. What made it bitter, and why didn't I do something to make it sweet?

Please, God, please don't let me become bitter. I got him back. He awoke from the coma severely disabled. We kissed: fishy, baby kisses. His eyes were like a newborn, and he was in some ways like a child.

I never want to know what it's like to have a stroke, a kidney transplant, and a medical center that declares this kidney transplant a success. If a patient and the kidney survive six months it is a success for the transplant center and their statistics are good.

Adam made arrangements to change the time of his tennis tournament. Life marched on. Ron would have wanted Adam to play. Adam won the tournament; it was held near our home. Adam entered it, hoping Ron would be able to watch him play.

My father, Adam, Ellen, and I were going to the funeral home. I drove and Ellen sat in the front with me. Adam was in the back with my father. I know no one except for children who use rear seat belts, with the exception of my eighty-two-year-old father. He prays for ten more years of life. I know he will outlive me, and I don't care.

Irving, my father, can't get his crummy seat belt off. He is claustrophobic; his arms are flailing, and he is screaming to get him the hell out of here. He's scared. I have an appointment with the funeral home director. I can't stop laughing. I am close to peeing in my pants. I will not be making a respectable appearance. Adam finds nothing funny about this scene.

I tell my father that I will leave the windows open and the motor running while I am away. He will have air conditioning. We are about to go to the funeral home when something unclamps, and he is free. I am laughing like it is any other day.

We walk inside the funeral home. It smells like covered-up odors, oils, and formaldehyde. We are not orthodox Jews.

Orthodox Jews are buried in plain pine caskets, only making a small profit for the casket company. We chose a gray casket. I proceed to ask Mr. Scott, the funeral director, his opinion of the HBO show, Six Feet Under. *It is my favorite show.*

I thank God that Mr. Scott took the time to give me a serious answer. He didn't rush me into the next step of this process. He told me that it was an accurate depiction of a funeral home in the state of California. New York, he said, was somewhat different with different governing bodies.

Did he really say that about bodies?

I cannot believe that while we were making arrangements in the funeral home, Ron was being doctored up one last time to look his best for his funeral. I wasn't sure where or when it would take place.

I asked Ellen if I should try to get a lower price on the casket. She shook her head no, but I did all the negotiations on our purchases. Would Ron want me to bargain for a good price on the casket? Would I be forever wondering what Ron would want me to do or not do? Would he forever be on my shoulder, in my brain, and in my heart in a good, yet strange way? Would I ever know?

Emily asked if she could publish this piece in the *Memories, Milestones, and Memoirs, Selections from a Writing Workshop.* I was flattered and said yes. It was published by Author House.

I didn't see anyone outside of class. I didn't make friends. The writers had husbands, wives, significant others, brothers, and grandchildren that occupied their time. I went to restaurants and bars. I had a glass of wine and ordered dinner. I observed the dance. I watched older men fawn and flirt with younger women. They purchased drinks for them in the hopes of getting lucky or getting a phone number.

One evening there was a man in a golf shirt talking up his golf game. He was bragging about what a great golfer he was. He was speaking to a woman on his left. He was left with me sitting next to him. He asked me why the woman got up to leave. I don't know, maybe she had to be someplace else. He said this was one of the best pick-up places in Boca. I didn't know that. He asked me if I heard his conversation. I nodded yes. He asked what I thought. I told him maybe she doesn't like golf. I also added that perhaps she doesn't care for people who brag. He looked hurt and said I looked like a lesbian. He mentioned that I won't be meeting anyone. He was right; I didn't meet anyone. I was simply passing time, just like him. I was amused that he thought I looked like a lesbian, whatever that means. I carry aloofness and sometimes wear it well. I enjoy my barriers; they were put there by me.

I signed up for more of Emily's memoir classes. There was a short break between classes. I looked forward to more of them. I wrote numerous essays. Emily asked again if she could put them in her book, *Selections from a Writing Workshop*. I said thank you.

7

OAXACA, MEXICO

❧

It was March: the Ides of March. My lease was up at the end of March. I was driving locally, but now I had a thirteen-hundred-mile drive back home. I was not convinced that I would be able to do the trip alone. My son volunteered to drive me home and flew down. We packed up my car. We drove home together. He had me drive a little bit. He was able to drive at night. He lived in Merrick, Long Island, about an hour and a half from Westhampton. I was grateful for his help.

I drove home alone from Merrick to Westhampton. I looked forward to being home for about a week and then I wanted out. I unpacked and everything was living neatly in its place except for me.

My house was the smallest house in the subdivision, but it felt large and cold in early April. It would be two months until summer bared its warmth.

I called friends just to talk. I was not sociable. I called Marilyn from the Southampton Conference. She said she would call me back. I enjoyed

Marilyn; she was bubbly and excitable. I loved her energy. I wished I could buy some of it from her.

I was bored by my mishaps. I bored myself constantly. I was tired of retelling the fractured elbow story. There was nothing funny about the funny bone. The truth was the funny bone was not a bone. It was on the inside of the elbow; it was called the ulnar nerve.

I purchased a desk when I started writing on a regular basis. It was a year before the Southampton Writers' Conference. It was when I finally gave in and became a reluctant owner of a computer. My house had a living room and family room. The TV resided in the family room. The living room was never used. There was a charcoal-gray couch in it. I moved the couch farther away from the window. It was a large room. On the other side of the wall was the kitchen and small breakfast room. I put my desk facing the window with the back of the couch facing forward. It worked for me.

The desk had a nice view. I settled in and drove to Sag Harbor. I went to the outlet malls. I saw friends. I didn't write. I didn't read. I went to loads of foreign films at the Westhampton Performing Arts Center. I purchased a memorial stone with Ron's name and birth date. It helped fund the maintenance of the theater.

Marilyn called me back. She was excited, telling me that she was in a writing group. She thought there might be a writer's conference in Mexico. She would get back to me. She was taking classes in the city. She was renting an apartment in Chelsea, New York. She loved the city. She still had the house in Great Neck, Long Island.

I was curious about this conference. I had never been to Mexico. I hadn't been anywhere. I was supposed to go to Italy with my friend Kathy, but I canceled Italy to attend the writers' conference in Southampton.

Marilyn gave me the details of the Mexican writing workshop. She was laughing; her deep voice was overcome with energy.

It was to take place in Oaxaca. It was for eight days, and breakfast was included. In the mornings, we would write on the rooftop of the hotel. It looked like the three M's would be attending: Marilyn, Margaret, and Marsha. I did not keep in touch with Margaret, though she lived in the next town. The last contact I had with her was in Lou Ann Walker's class. Mayan Marilyn, Marsha, and Margaret became the "widows three." Marilyn must be in her seventies. I was fifty-eight, and Margaret was about fifty.

We would be staying at the Hotel Casa del Sotano. It was not far from the center of town. Marilyn would be flying in a day or two before us. Margaret and I flew out of JKF International. We had a driver who took us to the hotel near the airport the night before we flew out. It was a rainy evening; our driver was in his eighties, and, apparently, there was a God because we had four near-miss accidents.

We arrived at the motel, tired and hungry. We walked in the rain to an Italian restaurant. We had a glass of wine; the food was fine. We took a cab back to the motel. We had an early flight the next day.

The next time I travel, I want my own room, even if it is only for one night. Margaret was snacking all night. I am an insomniac. I set the alarm for some ungodly hour since our flight was for 6:30 a.m. I awoke before the alarm went off. I hopped in for a quick shower. Margaret was sound asleep. I would be ready, and she would have privacy. I packed my clothes. She was sleeping, and I knew instantaneously that we were going to miss our flight.

I began to bite the inside of my cheek. I looked demented and felt twisted. This was not the result of a dental visit where a root canal was being performed. This was nerves—mine. I paced the hallway of the motel. I listened to the morning routine of other travelers, showers, and TV voices. I walked towards the elevator, heard the sounds of morning sex, and stood mesmerized near the door. I stopped biting my cheek from the inside out. The urgency and energy transported me to the life I might have had. Did anyone ever listen to me having sex with Ron?

I wandered back to the sleeping Margaret. I knocked on the door loudly and walked in. "Good morning, how is every little thing." Be Nice used to say that. Margaret pulled the blanket over her head. I put the TV on and began making phone calls on my cell phone.

She awoke disoriented. I was furious. She fell back asleep. She was a virtual stranger, and we had to get to JFK International Airport. I am better at this alone. I am better at being alone. She rushed. She was upset. We both had too much luggage. We called a cab. We arrived at JFK International Airport with not a second to spare. We had to go to the special elevator then a shuttle train. We were on the wrong train shuttle. We found the right one. We were dragging luggage like we would be living in Oaxaca permanently. We arrived at our gate, and our plane was on the runway and we missed it.

The next flight was for 9:30 a.m. We missed that one as well. It was not the right flight anyway. I wanted to cry, yell, and consume large amounts of chocolate. I had never missed a flight because of me. Flights have been delayed but not me.

I was on the verge of going back home. The thought of another hotel stay was unthinkable. I wanted to be in Oaxaca *now*.

After I told Margaret I was going home, she looked at me with fear and disappointment.

"Margaret, what do you want to do?"

"Let's try to get another flight."

"Fine," I said, but I didn't want to spend another night in a hotel. She went to the booking line. I was glad that she was taking care of it. I wanted to go home and dream about my missed opportunity in Oaxaca.

She was excited; there was another flight, but we would have to spend the night in another hotel. I was not amused, but I said fine. She said the airline would pay for the hotel. We had separate rooms. We were shuffled by a shuttle bus to a hotel. I was tired from our misadventure, but as soon as I was in the room, I was wide-awake.

I still wanted to go home, but I pretended I was having fun. I was not a good traveler. I was shuttle sick. I wanted to put my clothes in a closet and pretend that I was settled, but I knew that was false.

I thought of the George Carlin routine: the one where you go away and make a mini-duplication of your stuff. You cannot go anywhere without your stuff. We made it to the flight in plenty of time because Margaret made sure it was an evening flight so she could sleep all day. I was happy beyond delirium.

We were on the way to Oaxaca. There was a stopover in Mexico City and then a small plane to Oaxaca, the city of colors.

The plane landed in the city of colors. We waited for our luggage. I found mine quickly. I checked on Margaret. She did not have her luggage. We spoke to the people there. We waited and wondered where it was. Could it be in Mexico City? JFK Airport? Did she forget to check it in? Two hours later, they told us they would search for it and call her. She gave them her cell phone number. I gave them the name of the hotel.

We shared a cab with a young couple; they were missionaries. Were they trying to convert the Mexicans to Christianity?

The sun had set; automobile lights reflected license plates with uncommon emblems and color plates, letting me know I am elsewhere. Elsewhere had a ring of promise, quiet excitement. I wore black—a quiet, colorless traveler. The city of colors, unlike me, had no need to color coordinate. Nothing matches that can be matched. The reds and purples, even at night, shocked and intoxicated the senses. The women wore their hair in long, black ponytail braids, flowing down their strong, short spines.

I told Margaret that I had some clothes that might fit her and would give them to her once we settled in. It was late. We arrived at the hotel to a standing ovation. We were a day-and-a-half late.

There was food for us weary travelers. Margaret called someone at the hotel, probably Marilyn, to tell her that we might not show up. It was good to finally be there. The hotel was lovely with a private room and bath… I unpacked and gave Margaret some clothes that she could use. The room was nice with multicolored tiles everywhere. It had blues, oranges, reds, and terra cotta pottery; some were glazed, some were not. It was a peaceful and tasteful room. It had lovely handmade rugs in turquoise, orange, and brown.

I began to think of the artist Frida Kahlo. At the end of the conference, Marilyn would fly with us to Mexico City. She would meet up with a friend and we would visit Frida Kahlo's home. We would also see the Folkorico Dance Company one night. Marilyn had plans to take us to some Aztec ruins in Oaxaca after the conference ended.

Margaret ran off early to buy clothes. Her suitcases were still missing. She was taking it well; I must say better than if it were me.

We had breakfast *al fresco* each morning. After we ate, we went on the rooftop. There were chairs and a long table for us. I absolutely loved the rooftop. The couple who led the group was Peter and Tess. Marilyn was working with them in New York. Tess had written a book and Peter was half way done with his novel. We worked from nine a.m. to one p.m. At eleven-thirty a.m., a waiter came to the rooftop and asked what we would like to eat. It was a coffee, tea, or hot chocolate and snack break.

We were free after one p.m. to do anything we wanted. We could have lunch or shop for bargains and goodies. In the evenings, there was a salon where we would read something we had written, but it was without Tess and Peter. I attended two of those salon events.

The class consisted of many interesting people, a professor of economics from Brooklyn, New York, a young married woman who created crossword puzzles, a librarian, an anthropologist, Marilyn, the Mayan professor, and me, a writing-workshop groupie. There was Margaret, a nurse, and a local woman who once lived in New York in her other life.

I was glad to be on the rooftop. The altitude was high, but I never had altitude sickness.

I didn't bring my computer. I brought my Mini Cooper journal. Every couple of months, BMW would send gifts to its owners like a compact black book for journaling. The cover of the book had a sketch of the Mini Cooper.

When I opened the book on the left side opposite the sketch of the car it said: "Over the ages, world travelers from Marco Polo to Christopher Columbus to Lewis and Clark have had the foresight to record their experiences in journals. And in the grand days of motoring past, it wasn't uncommon for your motorcar to be delivered with a journal tucked into the glove box. Maybe they figured that a machine capable of moving faster than a horse was certain to deliver a few good stories. Or maybe, they just knew that in the countless hours you and your car spent together, you're bound to come across some things that are journal worthy. When you do, take a second to write them down here because one rainy day, many years from now, you might find it all very interesting reading."

We introduced ourselves. We chatted for ten minutes or so. We were told never to use ice cubes. Our drinks must be in bottles or cans, no salad for me. We were getting ready to motor on with our paper and pen or computer. Tess asked us to describe a period in time and take the long view. I closed my eyes. We wrote while sitting on the rooftop of the hotel. I loved the rooftop: so close to the outside yet with a perspective of up and away. I sat close to the edge and looked down at the cobblestone streets where the dead Volkswagens lived. We were in the mountains.

So happy to be away from home: I am living my life without my twin-mother convincing herself that my beliefs were hers, that we were both liberal sisters except for the time when I was a tenant in her womb.

I was in college, majoring in English and minoring in tragic love affairs.

I think my first college boyfriend in my sophomore year was the one I chose to lose my virginity with. It was more important to me to lose it than to love him which I think I might have anyway.

Diane, my roommate, was Armenian. She, too, was an English major and much smarter than me. I was sheltered at home; I knew it was best for me to leave home. Clothing and dressing well was my heritage, pretending to be what you are not.

I made friends with the local outcasts. We dressed oddly; we protested the war. We liked poetry and poets. I didn't go home for Christmas break. I told my mother there was a special Christmas workshop that I was required to enroll in. She didn't know, it was fine, more time for them to be with each other.

I needed to cut the cord. I hated the cord; it was coarse and suffocating. My mother replaced me with Sam or Samson, the dog.

One day my mother was snooping through my notebooks on American poetry. She came across some of my ramblings: my poems, my creations that did not sprout from her womb.

"Marsha, you slept with Robert; how could you? You are never

to sleep with him again."

"Yes, Mom." I never slept with him again. I found others, and others found me. She didn't tell me if she liked my poem, my creativity.

"Marsha, I will not tell your father about this. It will be between you and me."

"Fine, Mom." Everything was between you and me anyway. My father rarely acknowledged my existence. Why did she say this was our secret? Life would be simpler for her if she didn't tell him. Did she think he would feign anger to find the thief of my virginity?

Ron and I married in 1971 in the rabbi's chambers. I wore a Mexican peasant dress. I did not have a veil. I was not pure.

I was grateful I didn't walk down the aisle with my father. I didn't want him to give me away. He did that already.

We ended for the day. Marilyn, Margaret, and I walked to the Zocolo for lunch. We strolled down the cobblestone streets to downtown. It was a short walk. There were shops, restaurants, and cafés. It was a tree-lined, park-like setting.

Margaret's suitcases had not arrived yet so she had been buying clothes downtown. There were children everywhere. They were beautiful. In the restaurants, they were wearing their finest clothes, and gave you chocolate. You gave them money. Their parents dressed them up to make some money from the tourists.

We were looking at the menu. We ordered a glass of wine and fish with *mole*. Everything comes with *mole*. It was a sauce that has chocolate in it. I was enjoying the people watching. Margaret was widowed when she was in her forties. The three of us wandered to the Zocolo for lunch one afternoon. I noticed Margaret rummaging through her pocketbook. She dug deep and produced a newspaper article about a man whose wife gave him a kidney. Margaret gave her husband her kidney. He and her kidney flunked life with an F. Margaret was missing a kidney now. I was curious about her generosity. I was curious about her being a nurse and all. I was tested at Stony Brook University to see if I was a match for Ron. I was not a match. I was blood type A, and Ron was the universal donor with blood type O. He could give to any blood type but could not accept my kidney. I was relieved that I was not a match. I ruminated about Adam losing his parents: I was selfish. I was not as giving as Margaret. I felt differently about her; I tried to imagine what that must have been like for her. The fact that she was a nurse did make it easier, since she was always seeing life come and go. She concealed her feelings. I was not capable of reading her. You only need one kidney to live.

I read an article about a man who wanted to donate his kidney to a stranger. He believed we were selfish if we did not donate our extra organs. Can anyone be that altruistic? Were there other motives? Can a person be that giving? In the spirit of former President JFK, "Ask not what your country can do for you but what you can do for your country …" or your kidney. Zell Kravinsky donated his forty-five million fortune and one kidney to a stranger. His relationship with his family was strained. His elderly parents thought his behavior was excessive. He did not want his children to grow up with wealth. "He discussed giving everything away to the point of poverty." An article in *The New Yorker* August 2, 2004…titled "The Gift." There was article in *The New York Times* about him. There is talk of a movie about his generosity. I read in *The New Times* about illegal kidney transplants where people from third world countries donate organs for a few hundred dollars. I read that these people wished they had more organs to give. Everything is for sale. The lawyers and doctors that broker these deals get richer.

I read an article about a man who donated a kidney to a family member. He needed health insurance. He was denied insurance since he had only one kidney. It sure makes you wonder about motives and integrity.

Ron and I attended a discussion in Westhampton about transplantation. It was a group affiliated with the synagogue. Jewish law permits Jews to receive organs, but they are not allowed to give organs. Jews are not allowed to mutilate their bodies, no tattoos or autopsies.

Something about this process fascinated me: transplantation, generosity, and trust. The transplantation hospitals were more than willing to steal Adam's kidney and insert it into Ron's sick body. They would have done this, knowing that Ron and Adam shared DNA. I wondered about the odds of Adam having kidney disease as his father did. Adam would be without a kidney. I don't know how he withstood the countless treatments and surgeries. Ron had a client whose son was killed in a car accident. The boy's parents didn't want him to buy the motorcycle. Peter was a college student at Queens College where Ron received his undergraduate degree before becoming an attorney. Peter was hit head-on by an elderly man. Peter died instantly; his promising life in politics was done before it ever began. Every part of Peter was donated; he was Armenian. Some lucky people received corneas from Peter. Ron and I attended Peter's funeral. Peter Sr. and Ron became friends. We went to their home and Peter made grape leaves for us. Peter and his wife attended Ron's funeral in 2003. Peter's funeral was held in a large, lovely Armenian church in Queens, the domed ceilings shared space along with photos of a handsome young man. Ron made a donation to the Armenian Church in Peter's name.

Margaret told me that the kidney specialists were explaining how Margaret and her husband were the model couple for transplantation. There would be articles written about them. They would have more than fifteen minutes of fame. Kidney transplantation would have their face on the cover as an advertisement for what can be done for kidney patients facing end-stage renal disease.

I was thinking that Margaret might want to collaborate on a book with me. She never mentioned it. I even had a title: "One did; one didn't. The cost of dialysis might bankrupt the Medicare system.

I began to worry about Margaret and her one kidney. I was looking for signs of kidney failure. I became a pseudo-expert on the symptoms of it. Thanks Ron, maybe I could save her life. She was a number of years younger than her husband. Margaret was his only wife and married late in life as well. She seemed fine to me, but what do I really know?

I felt like a fraud. I was not a kidney donor, in fact, after Ron died, I had my name removed from the organ donor list on my driver's license. I did not want to give my body parts away to mad scientists and ambitious transplant teams, waiting for me to be declared dead enough to insert my not so ravaged body parts into another home, in another body of crumbling health.

There was talk about a collaboration between Margaret and me. We were both widowed by kidney disease. Nothing ever came of that conversation. Margaret had one kidney, Ron had three, and Margaret's husband probably had three.

I found the rooftop to be my solitary place after lunch while Marilyn and Margaret went shopping. I told them I was taking a nap. I would hang out on my roof. There were young people sunning and playing; it was a delicious diversion. I doodled on my pad.

There was a rhythm to our days; we wrote in the a.m. In the afternoon, we wandered about the cobblestone streets near the hotel where the dead Volkswagens lived and flowers were sold for cheap downtown.

The women in the group wrote about prominent fathers that survived the Holocaust with secrets larger than the mountains. One woman,

Sandy, came down with Montezuma's Revenge from the water. You had to keep your mouth closed when you showered. I used bottled water to brush my teeth. Sandy was intellectual and serious. She was an anthropologist, and when anthropologists get together; they talk about food. We didn't see her for three days. She was not talking or thinking about food for a while.

Frida Kahlo found herself and lost herself in art. Her art was autobiographical. Her portraits illustrated her medical conditions, her dreams, nightmares, and hopes. She wanted a child. She miscarried; she painted her pain.

Frida's painting, *The Love Embrace of the Universe, The Earth (Mexico), Diego, Me and Xolotl,* is a painting of the Goddess, the Earth and Diego being held by Frida and the goddess like the child she never had. He was the unruly child that she loved. He had a third eye. She appeared larger than Diego, but in real life she was petite and he was large. Frida attended the opening of one of her shows. Her doctors told her not to go. She arrived by ambulance. She was put on a bed and four men carried her to meet her guests.

The first time I saw Bette Midler perform was in Pennsylvania. The stage literally turned slowly. A stretcher was brought to the center of the stage. Four men were holding it. An arm rose from the stretcher; a blanket was covering her. The other arm was rising upward. The divine "Ms. M" made an entrance. There was nothing similar between the two. It was the dissimilarities that moved me. Frida Kahlo had her opening, as did Bette Midler.

We housed Ron's pills in enormous plastic containers on the gray dining room table, drugs for pain four times a day or more. Ron didn't have any diversions. He had me. He needed God on his side.

He had delusions of being healthy. We all did. Ron had physical therapy where a harness was attached to his paralyzed side. The therapist walked with Ron. He held on to the railing with his good side. It was tedious and zapped every bit of energy from his heart and body.

When Ron was alive, Be Nice asked me if it was better to be her or my father. I knew that she was in the beginnings of Alzheimer's, but she seemed lost and clear at the same time. She was sedated and calm. I couldn't figure out what to say. I told the truth. I said it was better to be Dad; I told her that she had my father to take care of her. He polished her nails. He cut the little hair that grew out of a tiny mole near her lip. He put lipstick on her luscious lips.

She told me my lips were too thin, and I needed to make them larger by putting lipstick over the end of my lips. She had to look beautiful for him. Be Nice asked me one day, "What Marsha's name?" She asked me if my father was my father. Her expressions were sucked out of her face by Alzheimer's.

We believe what we need and want to believe. Be Nice never remembered the question that she asked me. She shook her head and retreated back into her trance. Her eyes no longer danced. In the end, Be Nice, the beautiful, looked like a little old man with her baseball cap on her small head. Her pixie haircut was not glamorous anymore. My mother, the Hedy Lamarr look-alike, was no more.

My father took care of his mother when he was in high school and then he had to drop out. He was assigned to care for her, to make sure she did not tug on her clothes and undress. His father chose him since he was the sickly one as a child. His mother was diagnosed as schizophrenic and went to the state psychiatric hospital. My grandmother was probably bipolar, but that was not a medical diagnosis back then. She died a few years after her hospitalization.

My father was ordained to be the caregiver of his mother. As a young girl, I remembered my father wrapped up, shivering in his army blanket. I asked Be Nice, my mother, what was wrong. I was told he had the flu.

He was convinced he was dying. He lived to be ninety-one years old. He had long stretches of time where he was OK. There were episodes of dread and panic.

My parents never told me the family history. My father reluctantly, cowardly, told me the truth shortly after I became a widow. He told me that his parents were first cousins. I was the only cousin who did not know the truth. The other cousins did not have children. Up until then, they had decided not to tell me because I was fragile and shy. They didn't want to scare me. Depression haunted both sides of the family.

My father's sister Anne suffered with major depressive disorder. She endured shock therapy most of her life. As a young woman, she met a man. Be Nice insisted that she marry him. She married him and they had a baby. Mona was an infant when she came to stay with us. There was postpartum depression. I was seven years old and told all my friends I had a sister. I had a sister for a week and a half. Mona cried all day and night for her mother. Mona stayed with other family members until her mother recovered.

When my parents married, my father moved in with Be Nice and my grandmother. Be Nice left high school when her beloved father died. My father took care of my grandmother. She lived with us for all of her life except for the last two years when she had to live in a nursing home. Be Nice visited her every day. Be Nice entertained the residents; she was funny and kind to them. There might have been a time when my grandmother did not recognize my mother, so Be Nice adopted others and brought lonely, neglected old people the gift of companionship.

My parents became close with Be Nice's middle sister, Edith, and her husband Al. My father worshipped him. They spent a lot of time together while I was in college. They had two daughters, Ellen and Judy. Ellen was about four years older than me; Judy was about two years older. Judy married Richard, and they did not live happily ever after. Shortly after they married, Judy required a hysterectomy. She had uterine cancer. The cancer grew and she looked like she was seven months pregnant. She died when she was twenty-three years old.

There were times when I felt that Be Nice resented me. She loved Judy to tears. They were silly and fun together. Be Nice was like a big sister to her. I was her dark, shy offspring. If only I could have been more like Judy.

My grandmother had passed away. I was glad she did not know about Judy. I wondered how such a thing could happen. I was twenty-one and she was gone. I selfishly wondered if it would happen to me. I missed her. I thought about her all the time. I anticipated a time when I would be married, and our children would play together. We would be like sisters.

My parents were supportive. They enjoyed Edith and Al's company. When you lose a family member, you lose friends as well. Al owned tobacco plants in Cuba. He smoked cigars, cigarillos, and cigarettes. Everyone did it, it was the 1970s. They all smoked as young people.

Al was not feeling well. He had shooting pain in his neck. The doctors told him he had a pinched nerve. They were wrong. He had lung cancer. He began to tidy up his business, dispose of it. Tobacco kills.

My father transported Al to his chemotherapy treatments. The treatments took place early in the morning. My father had a father figure and friend in Al. After Al passed away, he asked my parents to look after Edith. Ron and I had a baby boy shortly after Al's death. We named him Adam.

My parents did indeed look after Edith. They were living in Florida at the time. Edith stayed in an apartment condo that my parents bought as an investment. Edith was able to live there for the winter. My parents lived a few apartments away from Edith.

Be Nice loved me ferociously. She hated me when she saw signs of the blue gene hovering around me. She told me it was from being selfish. She stopped talking to me. She broke my heart. I would have to apologize for my bad mood and sullenness repeatedly. Sometimes, I was allowed back into the kingdom of Be Nice.

They were there for others. I went to sleep-away camp. I knew they didn't have much money. When Ron suffered his depression, we had recently purchased a house. Ron thought his law firm was suffering financially and we would no longer have money. We would not be able to afford to pay the mortgage. My parents told us to sell the house. Be Nice explained to me that they wouldn't give us any money since it would be a bottomless pit.

Ron went to a psychiatrist who told us that we should do what we could to save the house. We cut back and saved money. Ron was put on an anti-depressant. We lived in that house for close to twenty years.

I was sad that Be Nice sort of abandoned me. She, too, had mood swings and a temper that could propel me into my room with my door locked. Many a time I would find her in a dreamy trance, and if I tried to speak with her when the trance came over her she would say, "Not now." She looked disconnected but peaceful. Her eyes didn't blink much when she was in a trance. I don't know where she went. I forgot to ask her.

I had found a home in words: my words and the words of others. I had a diversion. I had discovered in words what I had lost in life. It was time to find a home with a roof that was mine to rest and create in.

8

IT'S ALL ABOUT GEOGRAPHY

I was ready as my fickle itinerary was being compiled, compliments of AAA. A friend told me about the west coast of Florida in Sarasota. I-95 takes you to the east coast of Florida. Basically, that was how it came to be known as the New York and New Jersey coast. I-75 was the road that Midwesterners, Wisconsinites, Chicagoans, New Englanders, and Canadians took to arrive on the west coast of Florida.

It seemed odd to me that the road near your home could be where you ended up for a vacation or winter stay. I think the railroad had something to do with the demographics.

I was grateful that Sarasota allows New York types on their civilized shores.

I took a trip to Sarasota to experience the west coast. I fall in love easily with different places. I fall out of love just as easily. I was curious about Sarasota. I stayed at an Indigo Inn in downtown Sarasota; it was a boutique hotel. It was modern and, yes, blue was part of the color scheme. It was the part of the Hampton Inn hotel chain.

It was hurricane season: hazy, hot, humid, and heavenly. The heavens showered me with pastels: purples, shades of tangerine, and peachy corals with baby blue. An occasional cloud evened out the palette. The Sarasota Bay showcased statues of ginormous proportions. There was the statue of a sailor kissing a nurse, *Unconditional Surrender*, which signified the end of the World War II. It stood twenty-five tall. A driver had a mishap, and it had to be repaired. It stands tall and strong now.

I located a real estate agent to show me some apartment rentals. I viewed three high rise apartments—all downtown. They were brand-new condos for sale. The owners purchased the properties when the market was booming. Some of the owners thought a quick sale would net them a huge profit, then the market crashed. They needed to rent the properties to cover the large mortgage and condo fees. The three condos were in the same general location. I chose the one that had a view of the sunset on Sarasota Bay from the living room terrace. It was a high-rise complex with a pool, Jacuzzi, and workout room. It had a movie theater, computer room, library, concierge, and, of course, a wine cellar.

I signed the lease on the dotted line, and it was mine for one year. It had two bedrooms that totaled eighteen hundred square feet. The layout was odd, but I wasn't buying it. The living room was huge; the kitchen was tiny. The master bedroom was enormous. The master bath was larger than the kitchen. The second bedroom could accommodate a queen bed and night table with no room to spare.

I was delighted and gave the broker a check. My utilities and cable were included as well. My lease would begin on September 1, 2007. It was mission accomplished; I didn't stay in Sarasota as I wanted to go home and plan my move. I was given the address of the owner of the condo. I would mail a check to her home on Siesta Key. I figured the check I received from Social Security would be close to the monthly rent.

It was time to put the house in Westhampton on the market. I gave the listing to a broker who lived in my community. She had sold two other homes in my subdivision, but she priced my house too high.

I began to mentally pack what I would take to Sarasota. I drove the old Gerda Volvo to Florida. It was larger than my Mini Cooper. It was named the Gerda Volvo by Ron. Ron's father married Gerda after Ron's mother died. When they married, Ron's father set up a trust fund for Gerda. When she passed away, Ron and his sister, Debbie, would receive the funds from the trust. It was enough for us to purchase the Gerda Volvo. We buy cars when family members die.

I would bring my clothes, pots and pans, towels, sheets, blankets, silverware, lamps, and dishes. I also packed my Bose CD-radio player, my CDs, shoes, and pocketbooks. A box filled with my writings sat on the passenger side closest to me. I placed it in a large plastic bin that stored sweaters and assorted clothes. I would cover it with an old sloppy blanket to appear as junk, and maybe it was but not to me. I saved many of my doodles from high school and college. There were large gaps of time when nothing was written. Those were the marriage and family years where I read to escape.

People looked at the house in Westhampton. Jenn, the broker, asked me not to be home when she or others showed it. I was fine with that. I never knew when to come home. I asked her to call me to let me know when I would be allowed back in my own house. There was a man who was interested in the house; a neighbor told me that every couple of evenings, he and the broker would go to my house and stay for a while. I told Jenn that unless he makes an offer, I don't want him in my house. Jenn informed me of a potential deal. A single woman wanted to rent my house for one year, furnished. She was offering a substantial amount of money. I was tempted, but I would have to clear out every closet. I wanted a clean break. I wanted to sell the walls, rooms, floors, and the roof. For that, I would receive a check and run away quickly. It would be a business transaction.

I arrived in Sarasota with my assortment of everyday necessities. My bed arrived. I had brought some lamps and small end tables from home. They fit perfectly in the Gerda Volvo. I went to a second-hand furniture store to purchase a kitchen table and chairs for the living room so I could see the sunset every day. I would need a sleeper couch for the living room to watch TV, and a place for Adam when he visited me.

I met my next door neighbors from Indiana. They were about to discard a computer table and book shelf. They wondered if I wanted it. I sure did. I separated the unit, and it became an end table and bookshelf.

I went to another second-hand furniture store. I found a light, wooden table with four chairs, and a sleeper couch with a palm tree print. It had bold and light green trees with some black in it. It was uncomfortable, but it worked. Sleeper couches were not known to be as comfy as a couch. *C'est la vie!* I purchased a TV and computer. I was set.

The closets were more than ample in the master bedroom. There was a "him and her" closet. I used them both. They had shelves in the closets so I didn't need any more furniture. I discovered how little you really need to live. It was sparsely furnished, but it suited me. I waited for my house to sell. I knew it was a bad market. Less is more, sometimes. I found it amusing that the condo was purchased for one million by Patty and the furniture in the apartment cost me seven hundred dollars, not including the bed.

Siesta Key Beach was a couple of miles away. Every Sunday at sunset, they held a drum circle. People arrived with wine, drums, bongos, and tambourines. There were ancient hippies, hula dancers, and children of all ages. Parking was sparse, but if you arrived early you would find a spot.

I didn't miss my house, my pottery collection, or my garden with the blue and lavender hydrangeas. I missed Ron. I thought about my new desk; I knew wherever I ended up it would have a roof and an impressive corner to inhabit with a nice view.

I swam in the morning at the indoor pool. It was empty, and I could splash with abandon. I used the workout room a few times but I was forever getting lost. There were double elevators for different sections of the building with many key fobs to click yourself in or out. I opted out.

I picked up a brochure one afternoon at the library, which was walking distance to the apartment. They held classes at the Y, a short drive from the apartment. The Y had a gym with various machines and ancient folks huffing and puffing themselves to wellness or an instant heart attack.

I was intrigued by a class that was given at the Y. It was called "Reel to Reel," a film class. It took place on Tuesday afternoons, once a week, from 1:00 to 3:30 p.m. We viewed esoteric foreign films that dealt with serious issues. Most of them were independent or foreign films.

I found some kind of weird irony in my choice. I was in the sunshine state but decided to spend the afternoon watching films. The afternoon was the hottest part of the day, so maybe it was not so weird after all.

We would view the film, the twelve of us seated like jurors. We sat at a rectangular table. Some seats were better than others. It was a classroom, and the TV was ancient but worked.

After the film, Joan, who created the class, would discuss some of the finer points of the film. We were free to disagree and make our own points. We were retired people who loved film.

The class met for five weeks. There was a week or two break and then I returned for more. Joan prepared with incredible diligence. She spent hours viewing and reviewing the films. It was a wonderful class.

She was a lovely person, and we became friends. We had much in common. We were both on Match.com, better known as Match.moron. Was I the moron or those that date me, or vice versa? It became a pastime, an unproductive one I might add. Joan and I jokingly penned ourselves the *yenta* (gossip) network. We discussed the men we went out with. She asked me what I knew about some man she was talking to on the website. I would tell her to stay away; she would go out with him and then confirm what I told her. It was a small, boring world of internet dating. I had become a serial dater. I was not proud of this fact: I also go through men like toilet paper. "I feel fickle, oh so fickle, it's alarming how fickle I feel! And not so pretty. That I can hardly believe I'm real." FICKLE.

It was somewhat amusing to me that the fickleness of my youth was back in full force as a senior citizen. I went on a date or two and then took a break. It felt like work. The faces of men on the computer were thumbnail size. I met them at a Starbucks. I looked around and found no one there that resembled the photo. His photo sported black hair, but I spied a gentleman with gray hair, thirty extra pounds, and approximately eight extra years. I asked him if his name was Tom, and, yes, it was Tom. I ordered tea. We made small talk. I then asked him why he put an ancient photo on the site. He looked at me with sincerity and pity. He asked if I would I be here today if he wrote that he was seventy-three. I told him, No, I wouldn't.

I also told him there would not be a second date. I didn't blame him; he was going for the long shot. Ron was like that too. He would always ask out the best-looking girl. If he was rejected by the best, he didn't mind, but I was honest in my profile. My photos were current. I told him that he wasted his time and mine, and it might not be the most efficient way to meet someone. I should have kept my mouth shut. I left and wished him luck. I took a two-month sabbatical from men.

I wrote an essay about sex in my sixties. I wrote another called "Me and My GPS." I found that to be productive. It was funny and therapeutic.

Joan and I would meet to go to the art theater in Sarasota at Burns Court. It was an intimate art deco theater that held eclectic, small-film festivals for the independent film makers. Burns Court was one of my favorite places in Sarasota.

There was a singles group, Sarasota Singles in Paradise. They held events in the early evening from 5:00 to 7:00 p.m. It was a meet and greet in local restaurants. It was wonderful; I met my friends there and afterward we would go out to dinner. I met Cork from Chicago. We both had Hungarian ancestry. We became fast friends. It was nice having a male friend.

Every Saturday morning, downtown Sarasota had a farmers' market. The streets were closed. There were fiddles and banjos. It was the place to bring your pets, and I'd see pedigrees and mutts with designer scarves and fancy hats. There is an organic dog food store on Main Street. I accidentally ate an organic dog treat. I liked it. The farmers' market had wonderful fruits and vegetables from local farms. They had mini-craft booths and holistic face creams.

I met a couple through another friend, Nora and Ari. They were artists. Nora is from Venezuela, Israel, and Russia. She speaks Spanish, Hebrew, and English. Ben is from Guatemala. He can remodel a kitchen, as well as design and create furniture. He can work in concrete or bronze. Nora designs mirrors and pottery. She sews and paints. They have created a home filled with unique objects and fabrics. The theme is fairy tale. Their home is a fairy tale. You will never see anything like it. They are on YouTube. They have hosted numerous private events at their home-salon. Some of the events were metaphysical discussions, art salons, and poetry readings.

The outside of their home was as special as the inside. The walkways were painted and designed with leftover tiles and out-of-stock paint called "oops" from Home Depot. They had water views, quiet spaces, and places to sit and meditate. There was a horse in the backyard that Ben sculpted out of concrete.

I called the real estate broker in Westhampton; all was quiet on the Westhampton front. The market fell asleep like Rip van Winkle. I didn't look at properties in Sarasota; I was familiarizing myself with the area. I would not be able to purchase anything until I sold the house in New York.

Nora had a friend who had a friend who led writing workshops. It was aptly named "Write It Out." I was beginning to get back into writing and workshops again. It was a slow start for me. I was falling in love. I was falling for Sarasota; there was much to love and I hoped that this would be my home. My infatuation with Sarasota was real. I hoped it wouldn't be short lived.

My gypsy tendencies were born out of my parents' restlessness. You learn what you live. Ron and I lived in our first home for close to twenty years. As a kid, my parents could not afford to buy a house. My parents and I viewed homes on the weekends, but it was simply an activity. I thought that was what you did on a rainy Sunday. Ron wanted a house while I thought it was a pastime. Ron and I had made the investment, but I found it painful to remain in the dead house: it had been lovely and wonderful when Ron was alive.

There was a time for everything. It was time for the gypsy in me to show its face. I felt grounded not being surrounded by my stuff. I felt young. I felt like a prefrontal lobotomy had been performed, without the zombie-like stupor. My memory of Ron was not totally erased but enough was gone so that I could move forward. I did not bring photos. I brought only what was necessary. I was efficient and practical. I was thirteen hundred miles from home. I resided closer to the equator, the hot, red-orange sun would ease into the horizon every night. The days were longer here.

In Westhampton, there was a large half-moon window over my bed. The moon would make an appearance and dance through the night in my bedroom. It was like Cat Stevens being followed by a moon shadow. In Sarasota, I had the sun. The moon was female; the sun was male.

I paid my rent to Patty who owned the apartment that I was renting. She called to let me know she did not receive the check. I knew that I mailed it. She suggested we have lunch. I told her I would bring another check, and if she received the old one to use it for the following month. There was a new restaurant and she recommended that we go there. I told her I would meet her there. She said no; she would pick me up. I said fine.

I was waiting outside the apartment when a red, Corvette convertible appeared. A blond woman waved at me. She introduced herself to me. She was tiny, adorable, and tan. She was in her late forties or early fifties but looked thirty-five. I hopped in the car, not really hopping, since it was a Corvette.

We went to Sam Snead's on Osprey Ave. It was about five minutes away. They knew her at the restaurant, and we didn't have to wait. There was a long line of diners waiting but not us. She asked me if I liked the apartment. I told her it was fantastic. It was odd that I was the first person to reside in it.

I didn't tell her that I thought the architect could have used the eighteen hundred square feet to better use. Patty let me know that she received my rent check. It was mistakenly delivered to her neighbor, as I had reversed a number.

During lunch, Patty gave me a little history of herself. I was a good listener. She lived in New Jersey. She had three children. Her husband, Larry, had been incarcerated for the last six years. He was recently released after serving his six-year sentence. My father told me to never play poker since I apparently do not have a poker face. My jaw dropped dead. I was wearing my sunglasses. Her husband pled guilty to securities fraud and a pyramid scheme in 1998. He was forty-two when this happened. He cheated thousands of people out of a gazillion dollars during a ten year period. He could have faced up to twenty years in prison—lucky man.

Patty continued her story. They all lived in New Jersey when this happened. She had her name changed since her children at school were being harassed. She moved her family to Sarasota under an assumed name when Larry was in jail.

I was glad that I had finished my lunch. I might not have been able to swallow. I wished I had brought my own car. There was more to her story. While Larry was away serving time, Patty connected with an old pal from high school. They hit it off and Patty was soon in a relationship with her best friend--a woman. Her lover lives in New York. It was a long-distance relationship. I assumed that Larry and Patty did not have conjugal visits.

Patty no longer shocked me. She paid for lunch; I thanked her. She confided in me some more and told me that Larry and her girlfriend get along quite well. Her children are fine with the girlfriend too. I was beyond happy for all of them. I was ready to go home to my apartment. She wanted to show me her house on Siesta Key, a mere three-minute drive from the restaurant. I was held captive; I was carless. We drove to Siesta Key. I liked her Corvette. It was a windy, lush road with the palm trees; the flora of a tropical paradise was intoxicating and suffocating. The road led to Roberts Bay where her house was situated. The homes were close to one another since they were on the bay. This was valuable property. Her house had many levels. A grand staircase that led to the upstairs was curvy and dramatic. There was black-and-white tile with animal fur rugs. The couches were enormous. In the living room, the baby grand piano sat nestled near real, indoor trees.

I heard barking, chirping parrots talking and cats purring and yawning. Six dogs pranced out of a room off the side, near the bay. There were assorted breeds: greyhounds, salukis, and sheepdogs. I was just about to get the grand tour of the bedrooms. There was an open space upstairs that looked out over the living room.

Last, but not least, she took me outside to the bay. There was a swimming pool and a cabana. The landscaping was tropical with hibiscus flowers and, of course, the water. The four parrots resided outside; their colors a fine contrast with the green of the trees. I was in paradise.

The six dogs were back sniffing me. I was tired and wanted to go home. They were playful and peppy and jumping all over me. Patty asked me if it was OK for Larry to come with us. He hadn't seen the apartment that she purchased. I said fine, and with that, as if on cue, Larry appeared. He was about five feet seven, lean, and had brown hair. He appeared older than Patty and it looked like he had not seen sunshine for six years.

We gathered in another car since the Corvette would not accommodate the three of us. I think she wanted to drive her Corvette since Larry apparently had an expired license. I guess he will be doing the right thing from now on. I was leaving paradise to show Larry his apartment.

We were in the apartment, and I wondered what was going through his head. I was in the apartment with a felon. I can only imagine how much the lawyer fees would have been to defend such fraud. Was there stolen pyramid scheme money hidden away in my apartment? I tried to read him, but I really just wanted the day to end. I never understood why Patty told me all that, but she did.

He told her the place was lovely and they were gone. I shook his hand and Patty gave me a hug.

My overactive imagination was working overtime; my thyroid was underactive. I was glad to be alone. I called my real estate broker in Westhampton; no one was looking at my house. The real estate market was depressed. I renewed my lease with Patty for another year.

I browsed Match.moron. I was wasting time, glancing at thumbnail faces of old men. I saw a familiar face. Larry, Patty's husband, was on Match.moron. I decided I was finished with internet dating for a while. I will take a hiatus from it. I might disappear from it permanently.

I read his profile; he didn't mention his notoriety or where he had previously resided. He didn't mention that he was married. He was a liar and a felon. It was funny in a way. I wondered how many convicted felons were on dating sites. In a court of law, you may be found not guilty, but you are not found innocent. I wondered how many of them I had dated. I was on sabbatical from this time waster.

I often wondered why Patty told me her story. I never would have known about them, since she had her name changed.

It was odd that we waited with so much excitement for the birth of our house in Westhampton. Now, I waited with anticipation and mixed feelings about the sale of the same house. Ten years was a long time.

I attended one of those senior dance parties. It was a Christmas party. Christmas in Florida was surreal when you are from the north. The weather was wonderful with no snow or ice.

My friends are in attendance; we will dance with each other. I will dance with Cork. I might ask someone to dance. It was just dancing; it didn't mean I wanted to engage in a conversation.

I had a glass of wine. I heard my cell phone trying to find me. It was more than likely eight p.m. These single events started early. It was impossible to hear anything. It was one of the brokers from Westhampton. There was an offer on my house. This was the first real offer; I decided the woman who wanted to rent my house was not an offer to buy so that didn't count.

I danced with abandon. I said my house was in New York, perhaps life was going forward. I was celebrating prematurely.

The offer was low but I was grateful for the interest in my house. I knew that from the start the deal would be arduous, wrought with anxiety. It's not over until the check cleared in my account. Jenn told me that the woman was divorced. She and her ex-husband were selling a much larger house not far from my house. It would be a cash deal. I accepted the offer. When I was in real estate, I learned that the price of the first offer was the right price. I would come out of it with a profit. She wanted to move in yesterday.

I called my lawyer and accountant, Marvin. He was a friend as well. He and Ron went to law school together a long time ago. He called the broker and did all the work to make this offer go through. The buyer needed to send a certified check as a deposit on the house. It would be deposited into Marvin's escrow account. Marvin told me Carol, the buyer, wanted me to be out of the house as soon as possible. I had an entire house to pack up, but I was not in New York. I wasn't flying to New York until the check that was going into Marvin's escrow account cleared.

The check bounced, and I wondered how serious this deal would be. I told Marvin that when the check cleared, I would fly to New York. I didn't want to be there without a deal. Carol called me and asked me if I would begin to pack.

"Sure, when the check cleared," I said.

There was a part of me that wondered how any real estate deals go through. This was the very first step of this deal, and there was a major hitch. I never tried to negotiate a lower fee on the broker's commission. I relished in the fact that there was a serious offer, or so I hoped. I did not want to jinx it. Marvin told me not to worry. I waited to hear from him. Carol deposited the check about ten days later and it cleared. I flew into Islip Airport; a cab drove me to my soon-to-be ex-house. It was January and cold. I had a lot of work to do.

I worked from early morning until eight p.m. I made piles of yes, no, and maybe. I started with the closets. I learned how to pack from Be Nice Bernice by osmosis. Thanks, Mom. I didn't have time to have a tag sale like the rich people do in the Hamptons. They hired a company and literally put a price tag on stale, ugly wallpaper scraps and unused pieces of dated shag carpet, as well as stained linen napkins, soiled placemats, and tablecloths. I asked my friends what they wanted; I was fortunate to have a friend who was a hoarder. She took many objects which she didn't need or had space for.

I actually had another hoarder friend Robert and he relieved me of much stuff but I felt guilty. I was friendly with his wife and she was upset with the clutter that he already possessed. I gave Robert a poster of a barn that was in my living room that we purchased at Crate and Barrel. A few days later I saw it hanging on the wall in his house in his home office. Amidst his clutter and ancient newspapers, the poster looked tiny. In my house, it was hung on a large wall and looked enormous.

Thank the Lord for hoarders. Hospice also arrived with a truck to remove many items to sell in their thrift shop. I participated in a hospice bereavement group and volunteered as a visitor for sick and dying people. I did that on and off for two years.

I hired a mover; they packed my paintings and posters for me. They were too large and fragile for me to handle. They delivered boxes to the house. I was living in a boxed-up world: yes, no, or maybe. The more progress I made, the sloppier the house looked. I believed that in the evenings my stuff reproduced by spontaneous combustion and there were more things for me to throw or transport the next day.

I was hoping that I would not box myself into a corner since the dish boxes were enormous and heavy. It was amazing what we accumulated through the years. Linen closets are one of those dump-it-in spaces. It became a sloppy mess.

I asked Ron's friends if they wanted his assorted lawyer *tchotchkes* and bric-a-brac that lived in his law office. They were not interested. We sold the office condo to a young woman attorney, fully furnished. We lost about $50,000 on that sale.

I cleared out the legal files before I left for Florida the first time. The basement was empty. A major feat, I might add. I found myself going downstairs to the unfinished basement, since it was the only space untouched by chaos and stuff. The cedar closet was now empty. The winter clothes no longer lived there.

I removed all of Ron's clothes from the closet. I decided which pieces of furniture I still wanted. I chose the pieces that I loved and could see with me in the future. I, of course, kept my new desk. I had a nice bedroom set in the guest bedroom where Ron slept. I gave away my twenty-five-year-old, modern, gray Formica dining room table.

I parted with two couches, but I kept the couch that we purchased as a young couple at Bloomingdales. The gray, wrought iron baker's rack that we purchased at Macy's outlet center I saved. The *Blues Brothers* statue that I gave to Ron on his birthday was wrapped safely and soundly. I had a large pottery collection and kept it all. I packed them in dish boxes. I gave away my deep blue dishes that my aunt purchased as an engagement gift. They were our good dishes that we used on special occasions. When we moved to Westhampton, I felt we were special enough for us to use them each day. I loved them, but I was willing to part with them.

Carol purchased my outdoor furniture. She wanted the sleeper couch in the small bedroom. Carol also grabbed a desk and chair that was in the room, as well as two small end tables that were bought with love. She gave me cash.

I had a tag sale in Westhampton when Ron and I had been in the house a year or so. It was summertime. I put an ad in Dan's Paper, a weekly, local giveaway paper that contained articles and weekly events. I put in my address and the time of the alleged tag sale. They lined up to pick over our stuff. There were half-opened boxes; I labeled the boxes with the contents. I believed all of the items in the boxes to be discards. I was sitting in the garage and a woman was leafing through the box. She found my small, purple, beatnik jazz man. I forgot about him. He sat in a purple chair. His black sunglasses hid his eyes. The black sunglasses were painted on his face. His lavender hat was painted on his head. His magenta lips were painted as well. He was a bean-bag beatnik. You can place him in any shape. His arms were limp; his bean body can bend to accommodate any position. It was the positions you placed him in that made him a beatnik.

When I saw the woman with the bean bag, I knew I wanted him. I told her to choose something else for free. She was not pleased; she stormed off. I heard her tell new arrivals that the owner, me, could not part with her stuff.

I laughed to myself. She was only half right. I netted two hundred fifty-seven dollars. I assigned Ron one hour of tag sale duty. He sat on a lawn chair reading the New York Times. People walked by, and he went in the house to find me. I sold some more items. Ron said he hoped this would be the final tag sale. It was.

Two weeks later and twelve pounds lighter, I was completely packed except for the things I used daily. Marvin was setting up the date for the closing. I purchased a round-trip ticket with cash in Sarasota. I called the airlines to make the return flight. The closing was scheduled for nine a.m. on February 8, 2008. My return flight was for five in the evening, just in case there was a problem.

I left out a few raggy sweaters for the return trip. I wore my summer shirt underneath the sweaters. I wore a crummy winter jacket. My hair was dark brown those days.

My movers showed up at eight a.m. It was a dreary, rainy day that could have easily been snow. The evening before the closing, I called Marvin and told him that I would not be in attendance as I opted to be with the movers. I was not needed there. Marvin was a dear friend and wonderful attorney. We had a power of attorney document in place, just in case. I gave him the routing numbers on my checking account. He would deposit the check into my account. Voila! They would have the structure, and I would have the cash. Marvin wanted to take me out to lunch, but I did not want to witness the end of an era. I did that already. The house was our home; I cry at weddings and closings. This closing would be a tearjerker.

Mini bean bag

Carol's movers were lined up on the street, waiting for my stuff to be loaded onto the truck. I received a call from Marvin that the closing was over. He was depositing the check. It would be cash the following day. I believed a certified check was cash immediately. What do I know? The certified check, which was as good as cash, took three days to clear. I loved Bank of America. If they held on to every home-sale check that they received, they would accumulate quite a bundle. Marvin told me to speak to a manager. I didn't have the energy.

The movers would call when they were ready to deliver my belongings in Sarasota. I went to lunch with my neighbor Robert the hoarder. It was only ten a.m. We went to a local sandwich shop. He drove me to the airport with my one suitcase. I felt a surge of excitement, energy. We said goodbye and promised to keep in touch.

At the airport, I began my strip tease. I removed one sweater and threw it in the trash. I discarded the other sweater and jacket in another trash bin. I threw the past in the trash with the winter frost. Was that how O.J. Simpson unloaded his bloody clothes? Florida allows people who file for bankruptcy to keep their homes. Florida is a haven for crooked pirates and thieves.

I put on some makeup. I combed my hair. I was going to find a bar and have a celebratory drink.

I felt grown up and savvy. I made the right choice not to go to the closing. I own nothing. It felt right. A fresh start was blooming and looming again. I never had a drink at an airport. I never sold a house alone. There was a long span of time until my flight departed at five p.m. I looked forward to people watching.

I found a restaurant and ordered a Chardonnay. I was not hungry. I glanced at the menu. *I will order something to eat later.* My mind was empty of thoughts, as if I attended a yoga class and was in that moment of calm when the peacefulness sneaks up on you. A clear sense of joy was sharing some time with me. I owned that feeling. It could be the wine. I enjoyed being at the airport. I was waiting to be transported back to the tropics on this drab, gray, February day.

Now I was officially hungry. I found another restaurant to hang out in. There were travelers everywhere. The suits were working; everyone was using their electronic devices. Children were playing with their parents' iPod's, Blackberries, Blueberries, and people were busy communicating with their smartphones.

It was time to find the boarding gate. I was early, but I wanted to plant myself where I needed to be. I was headed toward Southwest Airlines. They asked for my ticket and ID. Then asked me to remove my sunglasses. My driver's license reflected blondish hair. I was a brunette today. They asked for more IDs. I gave them my credit card. I was given my boarding pass.

I went through the metal detectors, but my one suitcase was being dissected and resurrected as if I were not who I claimed to be. I was led aside while they searched for something in my bag. I passed; I was free to board the plane.

The flight was outstanding; it landed on time in Tampa. It was evening. I drove back to the apartment in Sarasota. The Skyway Bridge was eerie with diamonds lighting the night sky.

I had little to unpack. I organized in my head where the furniture would be placed. It was a simple task. The apartment had storage units near the indoor garage, so the majority of boxes would be placed there, without any cost to me.

I thought I would be rushing about to find a place to live. I liked downtown but nothing was affordable for me. It was pricy and I wanted more than one bedroom. Some of the older buildings required many upgrades. I dreaded the thought of redoing a kitchen and bathrooms. I preferred something brand new. In order to find something new, I would have to live in a suburb of Sarasota. I knew that it was a ten-mile ride. I was accustomed to walking downtown all the time. The farmer's market was a five-minute walk. The library was a five-minute walk as well. Sarasota had the most intellectual homeless population. They were the first ones in line to gain entrance to the library and the last ones to leave at night.

I waited with patience for my stuff to arrive and live with me in Sarasota. The movers had a delivery or two on the east coast so they would call me when they were near.

I attended the drum circle for many Sundays on Siesta Key. I saw a pre-theater screening of *Slum Dog Millionaire* at a film festival at the Burns Court Theater. Everyone in attendance loved it. Most of the theater goers were from a film group in New York. I saw the movie with Joan.

My furniture arrived on time. I placed them in their new environments without incident. I had more boxes than furniture. The movers put the boxes in the complex's storage units.

I planned a Halloween costume party. I had a hat that my mother might have worn when she was twenty years old. It had an elastic band that went behind your hair and fake black fur like a bird. It was a Kelly Christy hat. I purchased the hat at the Southampton Museum flea market. It was irresistible. I wore my leopard-skin leggings with my hat, my custom-made costume. My hair was brown and long with a few light streaks.

My five feet one frame was shrinking as I breathed. I swam every other morning. I was about one hundred ten pounds. At times, it seemed as if all of my weight resided in my chest. I think Cork wore his beret as his costume. He always wore a beret when the weather cooled down in Florida.

I had a lot of time. I made oodles and oodles of stuffed cabbage. All my friends came in costumes. Nora invited friends of hers to the party. In New York, we went to an annual Halloween party. I was almost born on Halloween. I have an affection for it, or was it the candy? The party went well with many witches. Joan wore black and had a small black mask on her face. She looked very film noir.

The party was over and I wanted everyone to stay longer. I had fun. I hoped my friends enjoyed themselves. I gave loads of stuffed cabbage and cake away. I had many meals left. I froze some of the food.

I stayed up late like I always did after a party. I loved being sleepy and getting the house back together. I would sleep in the next day and have a clean house in the morning.

I felt out of place in the Hamptons. It was not just the memories; it was that the person who used to live there, me, was no longer one and the same. I knew that wherever you go you take who you are. There is no escaping that fact. Even when I owned the house, I was not the owner. I was a tenant waiting for my lease to expire.

I attended more Sarasota Singles in Paradise parties. I met men; I dated from time to time. I didn't meet anyone special. I went to the library and Hannah parked next to me. She asked me if I was hungry, of course I was. We had an accidental lunch downtown. We ate at Epicure Restaurant on the corner of Main Street and Palm Avenue. Hannah had at least three-and-a-half doctorates and spoke Sanskrit. We spoke about our lives. We both have only children, boys or men. We shared parts of our love lives and agreed that we both had mediocre sex in general. Hannah was divorced. She worked at the Ringling Museum. She suggested we fix my ninety-year-old father up with her ninety-four-year-old mother. Her mother lived in an assisted-living facility in Staten Island, New York. My father lived in assisted living in North Carolina. It never happened. My father died first and her mother soon after.

I visited my father on the east coast in Ft. Lauderdale. It was a four-hour drive to my father's condo in Ft. Lauderdale. I would arrive in the early afternoon. I took him and his girlfriend, Ethel, out to dinner. After dinner, we would go to the Hard Rock Café where they liked to gamble. I didn't inherit the gambling or card-playing gene. I left them to their passion. I wandered about the casino. I heard the clinking sounds of someone receiving lots of coins from a machine. I found my father and Ethel engrossed in their pastime.

I wondered when this party would end. I was glad that my father had someone to share his life with. I was just hoping they would become bored with the casino, but I was wrong. Two hours later, I found them, and my father was ready to pack it in. I drove them back to my father's condo. Ethel asked me if I wanted to go back to her condo to play cards. I said sure. We played twenty one. I accepted more cards than I should. I purposely went way over twenty one. Ethel would explain that I made a bad choice. I told her it was my hand and I would play it my way. I infuriated her on purpose. The stakes were high; I think we put in five cents.

We said goodnight to Ethel. My father and I went back to his condo. I opened the sleeper couch. I felt like Elaine on *Seinfeld*, sleeping on that sofa bed. I was tempted to take a muscle relaxer like Elaine did, but I had a four-hour trip back to Sarasota. It felt lumpy and grumpy to my back. Tomorrow was Sunday. I had breakfast with my father and headed happily back to Sarasota.

I enjoyed the ride home. I liked being trapped in the Everglades. It was called the river of grass. I turned on the Everglades radio station. They gave the history of the place. In the background, you hear the birds, tigers, snakes, and the rustling of animals through the brush. I imagined at night the critters singing to one another in their language of the night, love and dinner. It was worth the trip. It was a peaceful, stunning place that was touched by an angel. In the winter, the population declined drastically. I never saw an alligator, crocodile, panther, or nineteen foot long python on Alligator Alley. The first and only time I went kayaking, I was three feet away from an alligator. Alligator Alley is a stretch of highway that connects the west and east coast of Florida. According to the radio station, Ghost Orchids grow wild in the everglades. They are the most revered orchids in the United States and are an endangered species.

Again, according to the radio station, hurricane season is from June 1-November 30. It is a long season in the life of most butterflies. Monarchs have a life span of about nine months. The smaller the butterfly, the shorter its life will be. The average butterfly lives for about a month. Some live for one day. Hurricane lilies flower magically after the torrential rains of August and September. These flowers go by the names spider lily, surprise lily, magic lily, resurrection lily, naked lily, schoolhouse lily, and Guernsey lily.

HURRICANE ISABEL, SEPTEMBER 2003

Hurricane Isabel was the first hurricane Ron and I weren't together. Isabel became a tropical storm. The ocean wanted the land back. I wanted Ron back. I was greedy for Ron. Mother Nature was greedy too; she won. The day after that she became federal debt. She lives in hurricane history.

On September 18, 2003, Hurricane Isabel made landfall on the Outer Banks of North Carolina. It was the costliest hurricane in 2003. It was a rarity to maintain Category 5 intensity for close to thirty hours. Some beaches in North Carolina are named Kill Devil Hills, Moosehead, or Cape Fear. I wished that I could have been on a beach watching the storm surge, purge, and steal coastline, wreaking havoc. We were only honored with heavy rains and gusty winds.

Ron told me once that I was too wrapped up in weather, and I told him it was the only thing I could rely on. I loved him anyway for being weather oblivious.

I had a strong suspicion that Ron and Be Nice had something to do with what occurred that past week. Ron's kidney would have been one year old. We named Dr. Shah, the kidney doctor, Dr. Kidney Karma. Dr. Shah told us the donor was a young woman. I hoped you would get in touch with your feminine side. We laughed; it felt good

I can see Ron standing tall, towering over my petite frame. His arms are embracing me, protecting me, and loving me forever. Ron was wearing tennis shorts and shirt with his uneven auburn brown mustache that I loved to kiss. He had nice, long, and lean legs that sported a powerful serve with a hitch sometimes.

HURRICANE PREPAREDNESS

I ended up on the hurricane committee in Patty's apartment in Sarasota. It was May; the beginning of the hurricane season. We would meet to discuss our plans in the case of a hurricane event. The other members of the group assumed I was an owner, not a lowly renter. I was a newbie to hurricanes. I listened to the plans.

We were advised to purchase something called a bladder. I am serious. You fill water from your bathtub into this device so you will have clean water for drinking and bathing. This thing resides in your bathtub. If it springs a leak, you can sue the company at a much later date. There was another one called a water bob.

The next topic of the meeting was looting. Since we would be powerless, literally and figuratively, we were informed that we needed to be concerned with that problem. One couple who possessed two large, smelly poodles discussed the need for weapons. I assumed that they had many stinky guns. I thought I was hallucinating. I remained quiet and nauseous in my seat. My head told me this meeting was over.

I faked a sneeze; I coughed a bit. I told the committee members I thought it best that I leave. I didn't want anyone to catch my fake sneeze.

I returned to the apartment. I decided to retrieve my AAA large print map of the United States. A restless feeling was coming over me. I felt a trip was in the works. I opened the map. I remembered as a kid that I had made up a game called Globe. I played this with my elementary school friends: Andrea, Linda, and Arlene. While spinning the globe with our eyes closed, we would place a finger on some part of the globe as it was beginning to slow down. Whatever country or city our finger landed on as the globe stopped we would have to talk about that location, dance a dance, or create a costume for that locale. If it was the ocean, then you had a do over.

It was beginning to become all too familiar. I might as well just spin the globe and take my chances.

I pondered my next move. I had wonderful friends in Sarasota. I remembered when I visited my cousin in Albuquerque, New Mexico. After we watched the annual balloon festival, I traveled on to Taos, New Mexico. I drove for miles, the mountains rising in grandeur and awesomeness. I was small; the mountains were orange and grey. The sky was silent and endless. The mountains steal your light and create shadows that cool and protect you.

I was staying in Taos, an ancient, hippie cowboy town. I knew Woodstock, New York. This was another dimension. I met a man and we had a drink together. He told me that I should check out Asheville, North Carolina. My trip to Taos was many years ago. He was a handsome stranger and what he said remained planted in my brain for future reference.

9

ASHEVILLE, ASHVEGAS, ASHVEGAN

❦

Asheville, North Carolina was seven hundred miles from Sarasota. The drive would be about ten-and-a-half hours. The days were long and humid. I would have the light with me. I told my friends I was going on a journey to the mountains. The stillness of the heat created a restlessness in me. A road trip and change of scenery might be in order.

I packed up a week's worth of clothes. I made a reservation at a Renaissance Hotel, walking distance to downtown Asheville.

I drove through Orlando, St. Augustine, Savannah, and Charleston. I spent the night in Savannah since I was tired and didn't want to do the trip in one day. I-26 leads you right into Asheville. I was on the road in the early morning. When the sun comes up the fog evaporated. It was photo worthy, but I stopped taking pictures.

There were flowers everywhere near the highway and the mountains; it was a wonderful welcome for the weary traveler.

A *halfback*, according to *The Urban Dictionary*, is "a person originally from the northeastern U.S. who retires to Florida, only later to move halfway back to the southern Appalachian mountains." I was not sure what a *Floridiot* meant, but it might be similar to halfback. I was becoming proficient at this pastime. I settled into the hotel. Hannah gave me the name of a real estate broker. I thought that I will spend some time here and let the city direct me.

There was music in the streets. There were mimes, jugglers, beggars, and pickpockets. There were folks who were picketing. There was a mountain breeze, and I noticed a small, independent movie theater on Biltmore Avenue. I was hungry. I had lunch in a breakfast place. I picked up a paper called the *Mountain Xpress*. It was a give-away newspaper, with all that you needed to know about Asheville.

Asheville reminded me of a smaller San Francisco, but it also felt a bit like West Fourth Street in the Village in Manhattan.

I walked around after I had eaten. It was a compact, lively city. It was a destination place loaded with tourists.

I went back to the hotel and rested. I glanced at the Mountain Xpress. Biltmore Avenue is the main street in town. It becomes Merrimon Avenue as you leave the city. There was a real estate section in the back of the newspaper. I debated whether I should contact Hannah's friend, the broker, who was her first boyfriend or check out the ads. There were numerous apartments to rent in the newspaper. Many owners, like those in Sarasota, needed tenants since they too were not able to sell the condos for profit quickly.

I figured I would call the apartments that were available. Tonight would be a fine night to explore Asheville. I would take myself out for a nice dinner. I could walk to most restaurants.

I found a French restaurant on Lexington Avenue. There is a Lexington Avenue in Manhattan. The name of the restaurant was Bouchon, which served French comfort food. The restaurant was narrow with a patio outside. I sat at the bar. I ordered a Riesling and *poulet roti au thyme,* dusted roast chicken with vegetables and *frites,* or potatoes. The food was outstanding; the *frites* were served in a paper cone. I was able to view the grease on the cone with perfection. I spoke to the woman seated next to me. She told me this was one of her favorite places. I was not surprised.

I walked back to the hotel. There were musicians in the street and music in my head. On Fridays at five p.m., Asheville has a drum circle on Patton Avenue. There were phone calls to be made to view the apartments.

I was determined to view as many apartments as I could. The weather was incredible; days were in the seventies and the evenings cooled off. The mountains created a cozy, closed in, and open breeze that made me think of summer camp. Friends of mine that lived in Florida sent their children to sleep-away camps in Hendersonville, a few towns over. I guess it was like New Yorkers and the Catskill Mountains. Asheville was more appealing to me than the Catskills.

I was lucky, I could see them all in one day. I met with the agent who handled the rentals for the owners. One of the agents showed me two apartments. The agent was meeting me at the third place.

The first apartment was a high-rise on Market street downtown. It had one bedroom and what they called an in-law suite: a room without a door, closet, or window. It was really an alcove, or a large closet without a door. It had a fine view of the city, but I didn't love it. It was small, and I had a hard time finding the kitchen: it was hiding near the alcove in plain sight. I didn't cook much, but I enjoyed eating take-out at home. The next one was on Church Avenue since it was near the church.

This, too, was downtown within walking distance to everything. It was a short walk to the fine arts theater. It was an older building. It reminded me of many of the Queens apartments I lived in as a kid. It was a two bedroom; the size was fine. The agent received a call while I was looking at the Church Avenue apartment. The next one I walked to and met the agent there. The apartment was on Biltmore Avenue, next door to the fine arts center. The agent told me that the building had been renovated a few years back.

It originally housed a plumbing supply company. It was a building with fourteen apartments. He showed me the two-bedroom apartment on the second floor. Many of the walls were brick, redone to retain the flavor of its history. The floors were dark wood with modern lighting. The bathrooms were redone. The countertops were concrete with a glazed surface. There was a wine cooler in the kitchen. There was an indoor parking garage. The agent told me that he and his wife lived in the building. They had a duplex on the third and fourth floor of the building. He was the unofficial mayor of Asheville. He was a sweet man and gave me a tour of his apartment. He had a panoramic view of the city. I signed on the dotted line. I had a one-year lease. I did not have any views, but it was fine.

I lived in OPA's, other people's apartments… when we lived on Long Island. There was a man who owned a company, aptly named OPM. It stood for other people's money. He spent some time away from home in a penitentiary.

My work was done. I was pleased; I was booked, so to speak, for a year. I gained a reprieve in some way of making any housing decisions for a bit.

I walked around Asheville with my lease in my pocketbook. I wondered what my Sarasota friends would think about my decision. They knew I was restless. They had lived in Florida for long periods of time. They were used to hurricane season. Maybe they, too, felt like I did but stuck it through. I knew I had made amazing friends and hoped we would still remain friends. I spent the evening at the hotel and drove back to Sarasota. It was a brutally long drive back, all done in one day.

I had a lot of work to do when I returned. I had to hire movers. I would get three estimates. I would usually go with the mid-priced one. If it was too low then they just wanted your business and there would be extra costs later. The high-priced one was a maverick that would lower the price, sometimes, if they thought they might lose the sale.

I contracted a mover. I began the dance again. I never hung a picture on the walls in Sarasota. All of my paintings and posters were packed safely in the storage bins, waiting for their fickle owner to transport them to a new place. The movers delivered boxes, and I boxed the kitchen stuff. I gave many things away again. I was shrinking the inventory.

I told my friends about the move. They seemed to accept it, even if they did not understand my restlessness. I don't totally understand it so why should they?

Nora and Ben asked me to make a list of my friends and invite them to their fairy tale home in Sarasota. They were throwing a farewell party for me. I was touched and delighted. I must be a bit insane to make such wonderful friends and then leave them. A part of me thought I was making a mistake; another part of me felt like a new adventure was awaiting me. The deed was done, the lease was signed, and the money was transferred.

I went to the butterfly sanctuary in Nokomis. I was beginning to say goodbye to Sarasota. I visited the Selby Botanical Gardens and wandered around. I would like my ashes placed there. I don't think that would be allowed; my remains might pollute the delicate balance of the gardens. I could always have my remains scattered at Nora and Ben's home. I was moving. I wasn't dying.

Sunday at two p.m. was the fairy-tale, *au revoir* party. Nora invited many of her friends. Her friends would be my friends. Some people are so possessive of their friends that they don't share. Nora and Ben were not like that.

Her parties were as terrific as she is. She was a phenomenal cook. There were paninis and crepes; she made us any kind of panini we wanted. The crepes were fantastic. Their home was overflowing with friends, and I felt such happiness for having terrific people in my life. Ronda was there. She told me I could send my writings to her e-mail address and we could have e-mail classes. I thought that was a great idea. I still did not know how to cut and paste. I was hopeful. It was a perfect day.

I would be leaving in a few days. I planned to stay with Nora and Ben as the movers emptied the apartment, as I was sort of homeless. I loaded my car with my valuables, my box of words in a large, see-through, plastic, sweater-garment bag sitting next to me in the car. I brought clothes since I wasn't positive when the movers would show up. I purchased an air-bed to sleep on until I purchased a new bed.

I took Nora and Ben out to dinner the evening I stayed at their home. I left their house early. I had to be in Asheville by seven p.m. to get the key to the apartment.

The drive was monotonous, but I was on a mission. I would call the wife of the agent and she would meet me by the garage of the building to give me the keys and remote for the garage. I made good time.

I was totally not looking forward to sleeping on an air mattress. However, I was looking forward to residing in the loft without the clutter of my stuff for a while.

I met with the wife, Rita. She gave me the keys I needed. Rita told me which parking spot came with the apartment. I was set. I brought my Bose CD-radio player, as well as my numerous CDs. I transported the items from the car: towels, sheets, clothes, and my box of words. There was a shopping cart in the underground garage for the tenants to bring groceries to their apartments. I put the air mattress in the cart. I locked the car. I was in the elevator on the way to Apartment 201.

There was a restaurant, Bok Choy, across the street from the apartment. I went there for a quick snack. I needed to get the air mattress pumped up to pretend it was a bed. I found the directions in Chinese, French, Spanish, and English, which was on the last page of the manual. I proceeded to pump it up; it had a manual pump. I should have bought the electric pump. After about an hour, I was ready to call it a night. The master bedroom didn't have a window. The door had beveled glass to give you the feeling of light since there was a window in the hall opposite the beveled, bedroom door. Sometimes, I placed a sheet on the beveled, windowed door because the light that escaped was facing me head on in bed. Like a criminal, I became sloppy. I wanted to be caught. I made mistakes. I sincerely wanted a permanent residence, I think.

The air mattress was not fully pumped. I think I slept; there was noise outside so I shut the bedroom door. I debated my next move. *I will call the movers to find out what road, what state they were in. I know they have three other stops to make. I don't know the order or any of that stuff.*

I was glad I brought music with me. I was elated to be out of the car. *I might sleep in the car tonight, in the smelly garage where the trash cans were. I will try to inflate the mattress some more today.*

I rang the doorbell of a neighbor and asked if they might be able to help me. An attractive blond with short hair opened the door. I introduced myself. I told her my problem and asked if she would be good enough to help me inflate my air mattress. Donna gave me the tour of her place. It was interesting how different the floor plans were. She hadn't completed all of the renovations. Her space was more conventional. The second bedroom was a workout room. She was in the process of getting a divorce; her husband was making things difficult for her. He was not signing the papers. She wanted to buy his interest in the condo. She was waiting him out since she knew he needed the money. She was shrewd.

Her girlfriend was living in the apartment with her; the girlfriend was going to law school. She said sure; she would meet me in my apartment in ten minutes. In a quick, five minutes, my air mattress would transport me to sleep tonight. Donna let me know she owned a jewelry store in historic Biltmore Village. In the event that I needed jewelry, I would certainly look her up. I thanked her for her help.

I purchased a bed. I didn't take the mattresses from Sarasota. It was time for a new bed. It was being delivered within a few hours.

Three days had passed since I had arrived in Asheville. I was pleased to have a bed. It was the little things that meant so much. There was a large group of homeless people perched outside on a railing that was adjacent to the garage of my building. My living room faced the garage. I kept the windows closed though the mountain breezes were desirable. As the evening progressed, their voices bellowed and laughter was echoing in my place and space. I noticed one night that a van was parked in front of the garage; a man was giving bags of food to the evening people. When I viewed the apartment, it was during the day. They were not there. I was wondering how I was going to get a good night's sleep.

I called the movers; it went directly to voice mail. I called the home office in Sarasota to have them locate the movers and my stuff. I waited, not patiently at all. I read in the Mountain Xpress about an open audition for a play. It was a Reader's Playhouse, where we didn't have to memorize lines. I went to the audition to try out. I went for a walk and found a movie to pass some time.

John, the mover, called me and told me they were indeed in Asheville, in the mountains. They had a rough time getting up the mountain. It took them longer than expected to make their other deliveries.

"When are you coming down the mountain to deliver my possessions," I said.

John told me he would call in a few hours. My confidence in being reunited with my material items was waning. I received a call back from the Asheville Community Theater. Thank goodness, someone called me back. The director, Harry, asked me to arrive at the theater tomorrow at eleven a.m. Ashville is a late-rising city. The stores open at eleven a.m. or whenever. Downtown Asheville has only local stores, no chains. While I was living there, two chains opened with much protest.

I arrived at the community theater at eleven a.m. I was given a part in the play *The Playboy of the Western World.* Rehearsals would begin in a month. I was pleased.

I called John; he expected to be downtown with my things tomorrow at two p.m. One can only hope. I shut the bedroom door at night so I wouldn't hear the outdoor entertainment. I put my CD player on, and I wasn't bothered by it too much.

John called with great news; the truck suffered a flat tire. I knew Sarasota was flat, but the trucks travel nationwide. How could they not know what they needed to get up to the mountain? When will you be here? We were disconnected. I waited for him to call back. I expected to hear back from him telling me that he couldn't find my building, or my furniture took a cruise without permission to be with someone else. I was bored and nauseous. I was ready for a nap. I fell asleep in moments. I kept my cell phone near me, waiting for John to call. I dreamed I was in Sarasota. I dreamed I was in Westhampton. When I awoke, I wasn't sure where I was. In the past years that has happened frequently since I have moved from place to place so often. I was in Asheville for one week and it felt like one week.

John called and hoped to be at my building by four p.m. It was three p.m. I was ready. It was four-thirty p.m. and they still had not arrived. He called to tell me he was not sure how to get to my apartment. I gave him the address. Isn't that what movers do? They pack your stuff and drive it to your location, and for that you give them a sum of money. If it was interstate, then you gave them a lot of money.

I was furious. I asked him to call me when he was on Biltmore Avenue. I went to get food. It might be a long night, or maybe they will show up in a week or two. I was thirteen seconds away from not caring.

He called at about seven p.m. to tell me he was on Biltmore Avenue. Biltmore Avenue was a narrow, busy street with shops, restaurants, museums, and street performers. I left the apartment and there they were. He asked me where he could park the truck.

I had no idea. John made a right-hand turn just in front of my building. The street was narrow. The homeless men outside my apartment building were waiting for the daily food deliveries. The moving truck was a semi-truck. As he made the turn, the truck made contact with the building next door that housed an art gallery. The truck was stuck and the wheels were spinning. The homeless men were helping direct the driver. Each one of them was yelling for the driver to do something different; turn the baby that way, no, just put it in reverse now. A crowd assembled; it became a circus. Where were the jugglers when you needed them?

John said he needed a new tire or two, after the collision. He had to hire a tow company to pull his truck away from the building. He told me he had no money, and asked if I would pay for the tires and tow? I figured if I didn't give him the money then I might not have my furniture moved in today. People were not able to walk on the street. In a few minutes, the police showed up to give the movers a ticket and advised them where to park when the truck was towed.

I said I would give him the money after the tow people showed me the bill. The tow truck arrived in an hour or so. They were able to back the truck out of the building.

They parked in an alleyway where the men hung out. They begin to haul my belongings onto a dolly. In about an hour, one of the movers jammed his finger in the cab part of the truck. They think he broke his finger. He was not able to work. They hired some of the homeless men, now part of the work force. I went back to the apartment to advise them where my furniture and boxes would live. The mover, who jammed his finger, had to go to the hospital in case his finger was broken. The truck driver's fifteen-year-old son was helping his father; he fell and tripped over a duffle bag belonging to the men that congregated outside my window. The kid had a bloody nose and elbow.

We were down three movers. There were three men in a cab on the way to the hospital. I hoped he wouldn't bleed on my thirty-year-old, black-and-gray striped, modular couch. My clothes were in large wardrobes. They removed the contents, and I placed them in the closet. It was ten p.m. It was going to be a long night. The elevator in the building was small. Only fourteen families lived there; it didn't have a freight elevator like large apartments.

John gave me the bill for the towing and a letter explaining the money I gave him. I sent the letter and bills to the main office of the movers.

The injured returned from the hospital hours later. The broken finger and the broken-nosed man returned only to organize, no hauling for them. I was officially moved in. It was one-thirty in the morning. I realized the second-bedroom window faced another building. It had two windows. I noticed this after all of the boxes were stored in that bedroom. I might have turned that room into the master bedroom. The truth was my furniture absorbed much of the noise. My TV was near the window where the men gathered. I watched TV when I was home in the evening.

It was over; the day was done. The men were very nice to me whenever I saw them as I drove my car out of the garage. They waved and asked how I was doing. I went for a walk one afternoon and noticed one of the evening men strutting along on Biltmore Avenue with a wooden cane. I believed it must have fallen out of one of my boxes. There was a box that was opened. The man looked at me and smiled. I grinned back. I was pretty sure it was my mother's cane. He needed it. I saved it. It was her companion for a short time. She graduated to a wheelchair. I couldn't bear to keep Ron's cane. Be Nice was eighty when she passed.

My stuff looked fine. I slowly picked through boxes. My clothes were in the closets. I slept most of the next day. It was Friday; the drum circle in Pritchard Park was a short walk away for me. I had *dunch*, which is a late lunch and early dinner. I ate at the Early Girl Eatery. The food was farm fresh, straight from the farm to my table. Asheville was a foodie place.

The drumming was intense, all sizes and shapes of drums. Both children and older folks were dancing juggling, and hula hooping. The aroma of pot was in the air; the police were there to keep things safe. There was a woman with Down syndrome and her hair was dyed platinum blond. She looked so pretty. She wore makeup and danced and danced.

There was a black woman who was the leader of sorts. She would listen to the sounds of the inner core of drummers. I think she was there to keep the karma exceptional and the rhythm right. There were tourists; I was a tourist on a year-long vacation in Asheville.

I was sitting on the concrete steps that led to the pit where the drummers drummed and dancers danced. A man asked if the seat next to me was taken. I said it is all yours. He smiled and proceeded to sit down next to me.

He was somewhat older than me. I looked younger than my years. He was wearing a hat. It was a lovely evening, and I couldn't stay home after yesterday's events. I had most of what I needed available to me--there were only two boxes of dishes, pots, and glasses that needed to be unpacked.

The man sitting next to me asked me if I was on vacation. I said, "Yes and no."

I asked, "Are you?"

"Yes and no."

I was originally from New York; I moved to Asheville ten days ago. "I am here on an extended visa." He looked at me; his eyebrows were furrowed.

"That's what it feels like."

I was an escapee from the northeast. We introduced ourselves. He told me that he was born in the Bronx.

"My name is Stewart, I live in Stuart, Florida, during the winter. I go north to Asheville in the summer."

"Is Stuart the east or west coast?"

"It's on the east coast, not far from Jupiter."

"If you lived in Jupiter, would Jupiter be your first name?"

"I liked that," he said.

I replied, "I lived in Sarasota for two years until last week."

He asked for my phone number and then went on his way. I remained at the drum circle for another thirty minutes or so and walked back toward Biltmore Avenue.

I neglected to contact Charter Cable services to set up my land line, TV, and internet. I will do that soon. I needed a land line to track the cell phone; it was forever hiding in plain sight.

I wondered if Stewart would call or if he collected phone numbers like people collect coupons. I planned to see what was hiding in the boxes that I had not used for three or four years, but not tonight. There was a place, Double D's Coffee and Desserts, next to the art gallery that was almost demolished by the movers. I went in there to buy some bread, cheese, and milk for the morning. There was a red, double-decker bus from Bristol, England. You can actually sit on the upper deck and enjoy your lattes or a malted shake on the upper deck.

I went into the second bedroom, better known as the box room or storage unit. I had no intention of hanging pictures. How would I get a nail into the brick wall? My black-and-white poster of Albert Einstein was out of the packed crate of pictures. Most of the walls were brick, but I found a single nail hanging on one of the walls. I hung Einstein to the wall. The black-and-white Einstein against the brick wall was outstanding. I tried to read *Einstein's Dreams* by Alan Lightman, again. I never completed it; I skimmed it, perhaps I was ripe for it now.

I lent the book to a friend. It took two months for him to return it to me. He returned it with the binder broken; it was a tiny paperback book, but it was back with me. I was different when I first attempted to read it.

I read in *Dan's Papers,* a Hamptons magazine, that Albert Einstein visited the Hamptons in New York. He walked into a beachy tourist shop and asked for sandals in his German accent. The owners knew he was Albert Einstein. They apologetically explained that they didn't sell sundials. Einstein pointed to his feet. He was at the beach and he needed sandals.

Rehearsals for the play would begin in a month. I was given the role of Susan Brady, an Irish farm girl. I can do accents. It should be fun. My part was not large, but there was some strange dialogue.

Stuart, or Stewart, left a message on my cell phone. I bet he does collect coupons. I wasn't able to retrieve the message. The reception was not great. I should contact cable so I can be connected to the world.

I called Stewart; he was unavailable to take my call but would call back promptly. He wished me, and everyone who called him, a beautiful day. I don't leave phony, cheerful messages on my answering machine. It's not my style.

I made an appointment for Charter Cable to connect me to the outside or inside world. I was never sure which was which. They would show up between eight a.m. and one p.m. on Monday morning.

Stewart called. Would I like to have dinner at Tupelo Honey? We settled on the next day at six p.m.

I had walked past the restaurant numerous times. It was southern cooking, maybe fried green tomatoes. I knew nothing about Stewart from Stuart. He knew nothing about me. I looked forward to dinner at Tupelo Honey. Ron's best friend was Stu from Glen Cove, New York. I wore jeans and a nice blouse. I wore my hat. I would suffer withdrawal symptoms if it were not with me. I arrived at the restaurant a few minutes early. Tupelo Honey was near the drum circle. I walked around the restaurant; he was not inside. I waited outdoors for him. In a matter of moments, he was walking towards me. He was wearing a hat. *We have much in common; we both wear hats,* I thought. He had a nice smile and I hadn't noticed his ocean blue eyes. He, too, was wearing jeans. We were in Asheville, 'tis casual.

The waitress seated us indoors. It was a bustling place with lots of people, waiters, and waitresses. We shared basic information. I was a widow; he was a widower. He had one or two other wives. I removed my hat; he did not. I think he was bald. His first wife died in childbirth. They had a son. He was a single parent. I thought about how difficult that must have been. His son is a little older than my son. He has three grandchildren. His son lives in Florida.

It seemed simpler to be with someone who had an understanding of the widow waltz. Although Stewart was widowed as a young man. He told me they married on a dare. Sharon was a teacher. Stewart said that if she secured a teaching job in New York they would be married; that was exactly what happened. They married and had a son.

I ordered the Charleston Chicken Sandwich on sourdough bread with Havarti cheese and a glass of Chardonnay. Stewart doesn't drink coffee, wine, or liquor.

I didn't ask questions about his wife's death. I figured if he wanted to tell me about it, he would. Stewart ordered trout; it was local. He told me he was a good cook. I told him I rented my kitchen out to the homeless men that lived outside my window. He grimaced and I smiled. I wasn't in the mood to discuss that. Stewart lived about twenty minutes from downtown in a condo. He purchased it many years ago when he discovered Asheville. Stewart was sixty-six when we met. I was sixty-two.

I felt comfortable with him. As a New Yorker myself, his being from the northeast was a plus. He walked me back to my apartment. I asked him if he wanted to see my place. He agreed. My curiosity about his widowhood prompted me to invite him to my apartment. I offered him tea. He did not drink coffee. He declined; I had water and brought him one. We sat on the couch. I noticed when he removed his hat why he wore one. There were a few long strands that remained, a reminder of what was lost.

He spoke about his son. He's a successful young man living in Siesta Key with his family. I told him about my tennis-playing son. It was a light, casual conversation that ended when I began to yawn. He said, "I'll let you get some rest." I walked him to the door. He put his arms around me, leaned in, and kissed me. I can't remember where the hat was. It was a nice kiss; he knew how to kiss. After a few moments, he said, "Do you want me to stay?" I said no but was thinking maybe. I smiled, told him I had a nice evening, and thanked him for dinner.

Rehearsals were beginning for the play. We rehearsed at 35 below, a tiny, dark theater that seated forty-nine people. *The Playboy of the Western World* had a large cast and that was why the director chose it. Albert, the director, was an older gentleman and a lovely man. He knew how to direct, and his wife Vivian was a fine actress. We did a quick first-read through to familiarize ourselves with the language and sense of the plot. I knew nothing about the play except the title line. A cold reading was a cold reading. Time, familiarity, and Albert's guidance would produce a gem. I enjoyed play reading and acting. There is something magical about being someone else if only for an hour. I get tired of being me. I am boring.

It was a nice assortment of people in the theater, like a box of chocolates--different and similar. We said our goodbyes and were told who would return on which days. My role was small; I would return in a week for three hours.

Stewart left a message on my cell phone with wishes of a beautiful day. It was raining. I attempted to make my day beautiful. I purchased a chocolate croissant.

"Hello, Stewart, what's up?"

"Would you like to come to my house for dinner Friday night?" I checked my calendar, nothing was there.

"It looks good for Friday. I have a GPS. There's a man who resides in my car; I have never seen him, but he tells me where and when to turn." Stewart asked me what I wanted for dinner and we agreed on salmon for Friday night.

Many of my friends would think I was taking a risk by going to a man's home that I hardly knew. They were probably right. I recalled family members who lost spouses at the same age as I lost Ron. They moved in with their families; they lived long, dull lives, dependent and depressed. I knew they were still lonely. Perhaps I might not live as long, but it was never about longevity. I lost my fear; I gave it away. I had a total hysterectomy. I survived. Some butterflies live for one day. I had given away too many days. I concentrated on the butterfly and its short life span. I had nothing to fear.

I never met a man who cooked, but I had heard about them. Stewart cooks, but he might not be a good cook. He mentioned that he was a good cook. Would he offer to prepare dinner if he was a lousy chef? I decided to bring pastries from the bakery near my apartment.

I wondered how the evening would go. The trip to his condo was about twenty minutes from downtown. His part of town was rural. I managed to make a few wrong turns. I passed his condo complex. I found it. I parked on the street. I looked up at the numbers, and Stewart was sitting on his front porch. I left my hat in the car. I would be driving home in the dark.

I walked up the wooden steps to his condo. He seemed glad to see me. His condo had two bedrooms. It was furnished in country mountain southern style. The second bedroom was an office den with a sleeper-couch.

The dining-room table was set. Stewart placed unmatched placemats on the table. After all, it was Asheville, Ashevegas—where people went to blend in, and lose themselves. The plates were mismatched as well. I liked that. He had a screened porch off the living room. We sat there awhile. He was honored with a mountain view and told me that every morning he watched the deer dance.

He found a bottle of wine and offered me a glass. It was early; I thanked him and sipped the red wine. Stewart explained the family photos on the walls in the hallways, bedroom, and den. He had included black-and-white photos of his parents, their sepia-colored history.

He removed a photo from the wall unit. He handed it to me; I recognized the face. It was a photo of Justice Ruth Bader Ginsburg and a much younger Stewart. He told me the story of his short marriage. His wife died in childbirth. Stewart would be the sole caregiver and provider for his son. Stewart applied for Social Security benefits as a widower, though those benefits were created for widows, not widowers. He contacted numerous attorneys though none seemed interested in pursuing his case. He attended a celebration of sorts at the local synagogue. He met an attorney and she seemed interested in his situation. She was a feminist before the word existed. She was beginning her career and had the time and interest to get involved in esoteric cases. His case had both of those elements. She was diligent and brilliant in her efforts. The attorney was Justice Ruth Bader Ginsburg. The case was won. The court ruled in favor of Stewart. The decision paved the way for future widowers to receive Social Security benefits to help care for the children. It was a large win for gender-based cases.

I found it interesting since Ron was an attorney. I felt compassion for the hand Stewart was dealt, and I shared with him some of Ron's medical issues. His tragedy was long ago, whereas mine felt like just yesterday.

Stewart was called to the kitchen; he had to check on dinner. I asked if he needed help. I was pleased when he said no. I drank some more wine while he put the finishing touches on dinner. The view was peaceful; his bicycle was on the porch.

Dinner was ready, so I went into the kitchen to offer some assistance. He handed me some plates to place on the table. We sat opposite one another. Stewart recently returned from a cruise to Alaska. He played bridge on the cruise and I played solitaire, rarely. Dinner looked good: salmon, asparagus, and baked potatoes. Dinner was delicious; my mind and palate wandered to the pastries. A good meal was not complete without a little sweetness. I helped with the kitchen duty. He cooked and I felt I should do something.

He had his own way of loading the dishwasher which was true for all of us. I am left-handed and load it differently than right-handed people. We sat in the living room.

"You really are a good cook."

"I had to learn since it was just the two of us. I took cooking classes; it was a place to meet people and learn to cook for my son."

"Well, Stewart, you mastered it."

We never devoured the pastries; I left them in his house. I gathered my pocketbook and car keys. I thanked him for dinner. He kissed me goodnight and asked to see me again.

"Sure, Stewart, just call me." I drove home; I had a nice evening. He didn't ask me to stay over. He tasted good. I wanted more, but I wanted time as well.

Rehearsals were beginning this week. I was pleased to have a schedule of sorts. When I arrived at the theater, we were given copies of the script. The principals in the play were there. I listened carefully to their accents. I can mimic language with some accuracy.

The play was about a son who killed his father. He becomes a hero in his town, but his father is found alive. The townspeople turn against the son for being a coward. He attempts to kill his father again. It appears that he finally killed the old man. The fickle townspeople are worried that they will be implicated. They abandon him again. His father looked dead but was not dead. There was a love story hiding somewhere in the script.

Stewart called and wanted me to meet his friends. He mentioned a potluck at his house this weekend. In our circle, we never did potluck. We would have parties and supply everything. I told him I would bring a salad. I purchased all the fixings for a large salad. I volunteered to bring it since I really don't cook.

I prepared the salad and cut my finger but there was no blood, just a tear. I put a band aid on my index finger. I continued chopping. The salad was done. I refrigerated it; I placed pecans, cranberries, and feta cheese on top of the salad and drove to Stewart's condo. I arrived and his friends were already there.

I met Rita and Sam. They were from Wisconsin. They lived in Asheville, deep in the mountains. Stewart plays bridge and Rita was his partner. Sam used to play but found the competiveness not to his liking. Rita and Stewart traveled to different locations to compete. They were serious players.

We were about to have dinner. I brought the salad out and placed it on the table. I was seated near the salad and noticed my band aid was resting in the salad bowl. I picked up the bowl and said that it needed more feta cheese. I went into the kitchen, searching for more debris. I returned and noticed two bottles of wine on the table. I poured myself a glass of wine.

They were a lively political group. It felt like Stewart was showing me off. I wasn't sure. The evening was pleasant. His friends went home. I helped him clear the table. I rinsed and he placed his dishes in his dishwasher, according to his plan.

He put his arms around me and kissed me, long and slow. I was waiting for the dance to begin. His phone rang; he said he had to take the call from his son. I told him I would go home. He seemed preoccupied. I was beginning to feel that ache when your body wants to receive the other.

We said goodnight. I drove home. Stewart wanted to go to a country fair tomorrow. He said he would pick me up at eleven a.m.

"What kind of fair?"

"There might be goats and sheep. They shave the wool from their bodies and sell it."

This was a first for me, the scalping of sheep. I remembered sleep-away camp; the camp was located near Forsgate Farms in New Jersey. We would visit the cows and watch them being milked. Our counselors would then buy ice cream for us at the farm.

I met Stewart on Biltmore Avenue. We drove to the fair. It was a short drive. We parked the car and walked around. Thank goodness that we were outdoors. The sheep were shaking and timid after the shearing of their wool. I wondered if it was painful. The animals appeared embarrassed and wanted to hide. The wool was placed in bins and later sold. We wandered about a bit. I was hungry. Stewart suggested we go to his place, and he would make us lunch, but I suggested lunch out. We had lunch in Weaverville. It was a cute town about twenty minutes from downtown Asheville.

We drove back to my apartment. I told him I was farmed out. I needed a nap. I asked him if he wanted to come over later. He drove home, and I said I would call when I woke up. The great outdoors tired me. The sheep were on my mind. Good night. One sheep, two sheep, sleep.

I fell asleep quickly, perhaps I should work on a farm. Up with the chickens and go to sleep by six p.m. I dreamed of cashmere, or was it Kashmir sweaters? I thought about being sheared without wool and being spineless.

I called Stewart and told him to come over whenever he was ready. He said he would be at my place in about an hour. I required a shower after a day at the farm and a nap.

I showered and felt good. Asheville was definitely a location with wonderful weather. The summer was mild. The mountains provided breezes and reminded me of summer-camp-night-air-memories.

I buzzed Stewart into the building. He looked rested. He kissed me in thirteen seconds. Sometimes, words fail. There was nothing to say. It was slow; it was pleasurable. Stewart was in the shower. I rested and maybe dozed off. The sound of the shower was comforting. Stewart was drying and humming some nursery rhyme. I hoped his humming would end. He was tone deaf. When I took a long, warm shower, I did not sing or hum. I was not used to anyone in my shower and using my towels, other than family and friends who visit from the cold climates. It felt strange and nice.

Stewart was ready for more and that ache returned. I wanted him close, I wanted him near, and I had not connected physically with a man for some time. I dated but there was rarely a second date. His kisses tasted good. Deep relaxation was the byproduct of intimacy. I felt tingly and sleepy. Stewart was not humming. Sleep came easily. I was not sure where Stewart was. I dreamed of nothing.

Stewart was sitting at my desk. He liked his emails. He appeared busy. He had been thinking while I cleared my mind of thoughts. He wanted to talk.

"Since we live half an hour away from each other, how about I bring some clothes over to the apartment?" Stewart remarked.

"We see each other on the weekends. If you want to bring some things for the weekends, then that would be fine. Remember, the weekends are when we get together."

He agreed and brought some clothing over on Monday. He advised me to close my eyes. I wanted to kill him. He brought over so many pants and shirts, it seemed like a move-in was in progress.

"What exactly went wrong here, Stewart? What were you thinking?" I created space in my closet for his clothes but instructed him not to bring any more apparel. I wanted him in my bed as much as he wanted me. We were like kids; we couldn't keep our hands off of each other.

"How about a movie later?" I said.

"I don't have hearing in one ear." Stewart replied.

"A foreign film with subtitles might be perfect." He apparently did not hear what I said--no response.

I purchased some serious hiking boots. On one Saturday morning, we went hiking to Grandfather Mountain. The views were expansive and heavenly. I saw a bear crossing the road a couple of feet in front of my car. I loved the views but did not like hiking. Stewart brought food, and we found a shady place to have lunch. We returned to my place. We showered and made love. I thought of my friends who slept in separate bedrooms and no longer participated in horizontal recreation. Some of my friends even confided in me that because of impairment, disinterest, or snoring they didn't have sex. We had sex in the afternoon. He was interested again in the evening. I wasn't able to fall asleep, his snoring was problematic. I spent my days yawning and napping.

We took a trip to Johnson City, Tennessee. We went with Rita and Sam. There was a presentation by Jill McCorkle who spoke about the importance of storytelling. He knew I wrote, and I was pleased that we attended the event. I liked his friends. I was tired. When I am overtired, I become giddy and silly. I could barely stay awake. I was laughing out of context. I intended to have a serious conversation about our sleeping habits.

We had lunch in a quaint restaurant across the street from the lecture hall. There was a one-man show at the Asheville Community Theater. The name of the play was *I Am My Own Wife*. I asked Rita and Sam if they wanted to go. They said yes. I said I would buy four tickets.

Stewart volunteered at numerous local theaters as an usher. He led theater goers to their seats and would then watch the show for free. He suggested that I try it. I explained that I like to be near the stage and concentrate on the play without diversions. They were having a meeting for volunteers this week. We would be ushers for that evening's performance. He wanted me to attend. He was hoping that I would like ushering people to their seats in exchange for watching the play for free. I explained my feelings about it, and that I really didn't want to do it.

"Well, try it, you might like it," Stewart pleaded with me.

When he met me at my apartment, he was wearing the attire of an usher. I wore a black skirt and white blouse. He looked like a waiter, and I looked like a waitress.

The meeting before the show started was to refresh the ushers' memories as to the rules of the job or task. We were seated at a large table. Stewart was speaking with a woman that he apparently knew. She asked about his children and grandchildren. He introduced me to her. I said, "Nice to meet you."

We were assigned locations in the theater. People entered. I glanced at their tickets and directed them to their seats. We had to remain at our positions in case there were latecomers. Once the play started, we could sit and watch the performance. Of course, when there was an intermission we were back at our posts to lead them back to their seats. Some people left after the intermission.

The final applause came. We were done being ushers for tonight. We walked back to the apartment.

We had been seeing each other for about two months. Fall was in the air; it arrives sooner in the mountains. My son was in the process of buying a townhouse in Pennsylvania. It would be completed by the middle of October.

I picked up my mail. It was about ten-thirty p.m. I removed my makeup, brushed my teeth, and put on my nightgown. Stewart was in the shower. I was in bed, faking sleep. I left one small lamp on in the bedroom since Stewart was in the shower. I breathed in and out, slowly, so he would think I was sleeping. He was in bed and began to gently touch me. The sex was good, but our sleep schedules seemed to be problematic. Thanks to his snoring, sleep was evading me once again. Stewart was on my computer reading his emails or checking the stock market.

"Stewart, I am making breakfast. After we eat, I need to go back to sleep. You can go home and catch up with your emails there."

"Okay, I will go home. Is everything all right?"

I needed sleep. It was Sunday morning; I had rehearsals on Monday. I purchased the tickets for the show when I arrived at the theater on Monday. The one-man show would be performed for two weeks on Saturdays at eight p.m.

I called Stewart to let him know I had the tickets. He was not in. The doorbell rang and I looked through the little peephole to see Stewart. I opened the door, and he had a suitcase and more clothing in his arms. He told me to close my eyes.

"Have you mistaken my apartment for the dry cleaners?" He laughed, but I was not laughing.

Stewart and Rita entered a bridge tournament that coming weekend. They would be in another county, region, or city for a couple of days. With him gone, I would finally get some sleep at last.

The play was coming along. The leads were fantastic. There were many fine actors in the play. I was having fun and passing time with words. In about two weeks, the performance was scheduled on a Saturday night at 35 below with a Sunday matinee at the University of North Carolina Center for Creative Retirement.

I appreciated the time I had to myself. I saw a film and went shopping. Retail therapy was a fine pastime. He called from the hotel room where they played bridge. I wished him well and said hi to Rita.

The coming week flew by. Rehearsals were shaping up, and I was hoping the play that we had tickets to on Saturday would be good. I called Rita during the week to see if she and Sam wanted to go to the Coffee Bus after the play. She said sure. They returned from the bridge tournament. They did well. Stewart complained to me about Rita and her game plan. I knew nothing about bridge.

Stewart signed us up for tango lessons. Tango has fascinated me for ages. Once a week on Wednesdays, we attempted to learn the dance. The dance teacher was the daughter of the agent who showed me the apartment that I was living in. Stewart knew her, and her parents. Asheville was a very small town.

He began talking about when he would leave for Florida. Stewart wanted me to go to Stuart with him for the winter. It seemed awfully fast for me. I wondered if the speed changes because of our age and the less time we have left. I was fortunate; I didn't look my age and felt like I was in my forties.

Stewart and I met Rita and Sam at the theater. They drove down from their home in the mountains. We walked to the theater. It was a serious play. The actor played all of the roles, both women and men. He was excellent. The play ended with numerous standing ovations.

We left the theater. I said, "Are we ready?"

Stewart said, "For what?"

"I spoke to Rita earlier in the week, and I suggested we go to the Coffee Bus. She said yes."

"I don't drink coffee," Stewart said with annoyance.

I retorted, "You can get tea, water, a malted, or you don't have to drink anything."

"Marsha, why didn't you tell me?"

"It skipped my mind." Again, he tells us that he doesn't drink coffee. It was becoming a boring, almost angry mantra on his part. It was chilly outside and nothing was happening.

I said, "Rita, I am sorry." We said goodnight to Rita and Sam. We walked back to my apartment in silence. The chilly air did not compare to the chill I felt inside my heart and head. We walked pass the Coffee Bus. I should have left him in the street to get a hot chocolate. We were in my place. I had nothing to say.

I remembered when Ron and I were in bed. "Marsh, I can hear you thinking, go to sleep," Ron had said.

I did not want Stewart to hear me thinking. I pretended all was well. It was late and I put the evening away; I cast it aside. I went to the bathroom to get ready for bed. Stewart would take a shower and that routine would begin.

He came to bed. "How come you didn't tell me?"

"Why would it have mattered if I told you? The bottom line was you don't drink coffee."

He was interested in some loving. He had an odd way of showing it. The dance began and I went through the motions. It was late and I didn't want a confrontation that night, or ever. He rolled over and the snoring began. I took a Klonopin. I doubted if I would sleep, but I tried.

In the morning, I made us some breakfast. We had oatmeal, tea, and coffee. I was a member of the play-reading group at the Asheville Community Theater. We read plays once a month, for pleasure, with no audience. We alternated roles; we played men and women. I loved it; it was therapeutic. Stewart said I was a dilettante. He wanted to do something else. He didn't want me to go to the play reading for pleasure. Stewart left after breakfast. I was alone, and I was almost happy.

My son's closing was inching up. The play would be performed in two weeks. When I returned from the play reading, it was early afternoon, and there was a message from Stewart. His message was that his friends were planning a commitment party for us. It was a pre-engagement, pre-marriage celebration. I wondered if that meant I would be committed to an institution where I would not have to make decisions ever again.

I had much to think about. It was Monday, and the week was mine. We did not have any plans this weekend. I had decisions to make. I consulted with Ellen. I forgot what she told me, other than to think about it. I made a pro-con list and ripped it up. It was stupid. I went for a long walk. I knew what I would do. I would call him on Wednesday. I wanted to clear my head. The party his friends were making was around the time I would be attending the closing of my son's house. I had time.

I called Stewart on Wednesday and told him I would be at his condo around eleven a.m. He said he would make lunch.

"See you later," I said.

I went to the closet and put his clothes on my bed. I brought the shopping cart from the garage to my apartment and started loading it with Stewart's clothes. I did not have to place everything in the car, just enough for him to know what was happening.

I was in front of his condo and he waved to me. Oh my, he will not be waving in a moment. I went to the trunk and removed as much as I could. He looked deflated and shocked. He placed his hand on his head as though he had been hit. I felt for him, but I knew I did the right thing. I carried his clothing up the steps and he said, "Oh, no." I said nothing.

Words evaded me. I deposited his clothes on the bed. He looked sad. I knew that I would miss him. He was in my life and we spent time together. He was smart, but I dreaded being with him. I would miss being occupied with activities with him, but I needed to go forward and leave him behind.

I was determined and anxious about ending the relationship with Stewart. I never expected him to take it so badly. I underestimated his feelings for me. I was selfish and didn't want to answer to anyone.

Stewart called me a dilettante and it disturbed me greatly, then, but no longer. I am a dilettante. I am alone and lonely. I might be a fickle dilettant.

> *Untitled*
> *I've had my fill*
> *I've had my fair share*
> *I am done with it*
> *Love, that is for now.*
>
> *I wait for no one*
> *I sleep when I please*
> *I've tired of the dance*
> *The triple step the tendu*
> *The stepping on toes*
> *The sharing of colds*
> *I don't want a one night stand*
> *Or a 2 year run at best.*

I have no interest in having it all
I've embraced my choices
I've embraced my losses

AH MEN

There would be no lunch for me. I said goodbye and wished him well. He said he would contact me to pick up the rest of his belongings.

I drove off and shed some tears. Beginnings were great but endings were still bittersweet. I returned to the apartment. I put the remains of Stewart's clothes and shoes in the storage room, better known as the box room. I didn't want any part of him in my sight. Of course, he was in my head but I was starting to clear him out.

The performance of *The Playboy of the Western World* went well. It was long and verbose, but it told of a time in Ireland where there was much upheaval and violence. Landowners were resented and the poor rebelled.

I helped Adam pack up his clothes, furnishings, posters, and assorted possessions in Pennsylvania. Luckily the young haven't had the chance to accumulate as much as the old.

I went to the closing. It was boring and not as long as I thought it would be. The movers picked up Adam's furniture the next day. I was tired from the packing and the drive. I planned on leaving for Asheville early in the morning. The closing was on my birthday, November 2nd.

Fall was approaching: it was stunning in Asheville with the leaves changing early. It was refreshing to witness the change. It was life affirming to see the cycles of nature.

Stewart e-mailed me and wanted to know how the closing went. I waited a week and e-mailed that it was indeed boring, but Adam was a homeowner. I thanked him for his interest. I knew I would never hear from him again.

I began looking at properties again. There were new homes being built in Weaverville, about twenty minutes from downtown Asheville. The homes were cottage bungalow style—sweet look, plenty of space. I met with a broker to negotiate the price and which lot to purchase. The broker was working on a proposal for me.

In the fall, I had assorted tests performed on me. They did bone density, mammogram, and blood tests. I considered it an oil and lube of sorts. My bone density told me what I already knew. I had osteoporosis. My mammogram was of concern. I needed to reschedule and have another one. This had happened before, and it was more of an annoyance. My breasts were large. When they were smooched down on the machine, they resembled pancakes. My pancake tits needed retesting. I found it hard to believe that they were a part of me; they looked weird resting on the machine.

The broker sent me a proposal on the property in Weaverville. I needed to take another mammogram. I called the broker and told her that I needed to put the proposal on hold until I received the results of medical tests. She understood, and I said I would be in touch. I scheduled the mammogram for the following week. I wanted a clean bill of health if I would be buying a house. I waited, not so patiently, for the results of the mammogram. I stayed home and relished in my ability to go to sleep early. I received a call from the doctor that my test was fine and not to worry.

I was glad all was well, but I didn't feel well. Thanksgiving was approaching, and I had a sore throat that was developing into a cough. I waited to go to the doctor, hoping it would just get better but it didn't. I developed a fever at night. I have had bronchitis many times, and it starts little and grows into pneumonia. It had been exceptionally cold and windy lately. I made an appointment with the doctor. It seemed everyone was sick with the flu and coughs. They gave me an appointment for the following week.

I drove to the supermarket to buy chicken, celery, carrots parsley, and noodles to make chicken soup. I won't have to run out for food. I can remain holed up in my apartment, dining on chicken soup and chicken breasts.

I found it comforting to stay home and wear sweat pants over my PJs. My cough was raw and sometimes I thought I might break a rib. I developed laryngitis; I rarely spoke on the phone. I sounded worse than I felt. The fever was going away, but I felt I needed to see a doctor.

This was the year I became addicted to *So You Think You Can Dance*— *SYTYCD*. I never watched it before. I loved every minute of it. The quality of the dancers was spectacular. I was content in my boredom.

I went to the doctor. Everyone was choking. I saw an elderly woman in the office who mildly told the nurses she had pain in her chest, and I watched her color fade to gray. I went to the nurses' station to tell them I thought she was about to pass out. They brought her into the office quickly. In about fifteen minutes, an ambulance arrived to take her to the hospital. She had suffered a heart attack.

I was not overly impressed with that office: how did they miss it? When I was called in, the doctor was maybe twenty-three, according to my old eyes. I needed an antibiotic. He gave me a prescription for Biaxin and cough medicine. I filled the prescriptions. I went back to the apartment armed with Biaxin, or something that sounded like that, and cough medicine. I drank hot tea with honey and cough medicine with codeine. The doctor told me to call him if I wasn't feeling better after I completed the antibiotics.

In my medicated state, I attempted to map out a plan for the rest of my life. You plan, god laughs. I needed to retrieve my AAA map from the car one last time. My living in resort-type places was enviable, I suppose, but it might prove to have been the problem after all.

I felt like I was running out of places. I was aging alone, but it was my choice. I went to the garage and found old faithful, my bible of late. My battered, large-print map was needed to assist me in mapping out this life of mine.

I have discovered that conventional wisdom is just that. No one wants to die alone, but you will die alone. I was at Ron's side every day. I was there when he left, but he died alone. It was not a communal activity. People may surround you with their love and karma but it was your death. Your breath stops not in tandem, not in sync. It is the trip of your life…the exit is what life leads to all of life's lilies, butterflies, penguins, and ladybugs.

I froze in the garage but I was on a mission. Soon I was back and cozy in my place. With diligence and codeine-laced cough medicine, I studied the U.S. I liked North Carolina. Something about it reminded me of New York. It had the mountains, ocean, and beaches. It had a city, Raleigh. There were suburbs. Many transplants from all over resided in Cary or Raleigh. There was Durham, Winston-Salem, and Chapel Hill. Ron's sister, Debbie, lived in Apex, somewhere near Raleigh and Cary.

After Ron died, I went to Apex from some other road trip of mine to visit Debbie, Ron's sister. I didn't pay much attention to her locale. I had many trips to take before I would be ready to think of living someplace permanently.

This evening, between coughing, wheezing, and watching *"So You Think You Can Dance,"* I fell asleep on my modular couch. I clutched the map and dreamt about nothing. I woke up because the TV was on. I fell asleep because the codeine knocked me out. I turned the TV off and drifted into my windowless bedroom. I slept on two pillows so I wouldn't cough as much. I fell asleep quickly. Mornings were the worst. I was congested; my head throbbed. I took my Biaxin with hot tea and toast. I made my bed even though I would return to it shortly. I needed some kind of order, especially when I didn't feel well. My throat was sore from my constant cough. It had been one week since I saw the doctor. I still had antibiotics left. The laryngitis was not better, but I didn't have a fever.

I was armed with my map. I perused locations and began to think, if I ever got rid of this bronchitis, I wanted to take a road trip to Cary, North Carolina. Thanksgiving came and went. I had Chinese food and wonton soup on Thanksgiving.

During the month of December in Asheville, every Saturday night there were fireworks. I found some pleasure in that, only in Asheville. I had completed the antibiotics, but the cough was still alive and well. I made an appointment with Dr. Jason. He looked like an undergraduate med student. My appointment was a week before Christmas. Everyone was frantically shopping; no one was going to the doctor. It was sacrilegious to seek help. The shopping wars were surging.

I didn't miss Stewart at all. I missed being busy. He occupied my time. He was the wrong occupant. When I went to his condo that last time, he said that he needed someone in his life. I told him I wanted someone in my life, but I didn't need someone. He began to discuss the difference. He was becoming agitated. I said I was sorry and wished him well.

I returned to Dr. Jason's office. He gave me another round of antibiotics. I filled the prescription and went to the grocery store for more chicken and vegetables for chicken soup. While sipping on some chicken soup, I remembered an incident back in New York.

I went to the orthopedist and brought him an x-ray of my knee. The doctor looked at it and said, "Thank you for bringing it, but I won't be needing it; this was your mammogram."

I blushed and then I could not stop laughing. The tears were rolling down my face. How many times can you have a good laugh at the doctor's office? I remembered nothing about my knee and how it was doing. I left with my mammogram in my hand.

I didn't attend the monthly play readings. It snowed; the weather was cold and dreary. It didn't matter; I stayed in, rested, and waited to get better. I dodged a bullet; bronchitis was nothing compared to flunking the mammogram. I began to feel grateful. Christmas came; New Year's Eve was the last of the fireworks for the year.

I went back to the doctor. I was still coughing and wheezing. He prescribed something for the wheezing and told me if I didn't feel better in a few weeks that he would x-ray my lungs. I drank plenty of liquids; I watched SYTYCD but no dancing for me.

I left the apartment on sunny days. I was winded during a short walk to the library. I felt better being outdoors. The sun on my face felt good. I tried to walk each day. The weather and I were improving. I thought I might be close to being ready for a trip to Cary and Apex. I called Debbie in Apex and told her my plans. She had visited me for a weekend in the fall in Asheville. She was excited that I was considering moving near her. She commented that she didn't have family anywhere nearby. What was she thinking? I wondered if she forgot that her mother died at fifty-five, her father at sixty-two, and her brother, Ron, died at fifty-seven. Her family had passed away. I was family by marriage.

I no longer watched SYTYCD. I loved dancing, but the show was Hollywood hype.

The dance was getting old. I contacted a real estate broker in Cary, Apex. We spoke and she emailed me listings. I viewed them while I was in Asheville. I was becoming seasick and house sick, glancing at all of the properties. I planned to make the trip in a few weeks. I made reservations at a Marriott in Cary.

10
"CARY" ON LUGGAGE

It was bitter in Asheville; it was warmer in Cary. I drove to Cary, a six-hour drive. I settled into the hotel. The plan was to look at properties the following day. The broker, Sue, picked me up at the hotel and gave me a mini-tour of areas in Cary. We looked at numerous homes.

The homes required work because of ancient bathrooms and avocado-colored refrigerators. I would have to renovate. I didn't have the patience for that experience. I advised the broker that new was what I wanted. She said that would be hard, but she would do another search. She dropped me off at the hotel.

My sister-in-law Debbie's husband, Bob, was unemployed. He had worked for IBM and planned to retire with a hefty IBM pension, but they beat him to the punch. They let him go. I called Debbie and asked if they wanted to come to my hotel. There was a restaurant nearby. Debbie said sure and we had dinner together. It was nice. Debbie was twelve years younger than me. She always loved animals and groomed dogs.

I needed to rethink the plan; perhaps I should rent again, live in the area and discover what was available for me without risk. I would look at the properties that Sue was searching for today, but my gut told me to rent and play it safe. Truly, it was not because I was fickle. It was because I *am* fickle.

Sue picked me up at eleven a.m. We went driving, and I discovered that Cary was a nice, regular place, not a resort at all. It was fine not to be driving. The houses were too large or too small, nothing seemed right. I took Sue out to lunch. She was hard working, but I thought it best to wait.

The following day when I awoke, it was exceptionally still like during the summer when the temperature climbs. When the air is thick, the humidity eliminates sound. I felt that again today in the room with the curtains drawn. It was winter in Asheville; it was winter in Cary. I opened the curtains, and we were in the midst of a southern snowstorm. I had breakfast at the hotel. It was a winter wonderland. Everyone was talking about it. Winters were known to be short and mild in Cary, but not this year. They were not equipped to handle snowstorms since they were infrequent. Schools were closed. They didn't have snow plows like New York, New England, and Buffalo. Life was suspended; people did not have the experience to drive in this kind of weather. I had my ice and snow brush in the car, lucky me. I brought boots just in case. I walked to the parking lot to my car to retrieve my sweaters and socks. I started the car, put the heat on, and started to scrape the ice off the windshield. I was bored so I went back to the hotel.

The schools remained closed, because with temperatures in the twenties, overnight everything froze. I drove to the restaurant that I took

Debbie and Bob to the other night. It was about five p.m. It was a two-minute ride. I drove on the ice. I had an early dinner. I wondered what the weather was like in Asheville. I wasn't sure when I would leave; I preferred not to drive in snow. I wanted to drive around Cary to find an apartment for July 1. My lease was up on the 30th of June, five months away.

I followed the snow or the snow followed me. I remained in the hotel for two more days. There was a heat wave, so snow and ice began to melt. I was stir crazy; I wanted to go home or look at neighborhoods. I ventured out to solidify the plan. I knew one of the main roads was Cary Parkway. I passed the usual suspects, the stores that were everywhere: Kohl's, Steinmart, Home Goods, Target, and Pier 1.

I found a mixed-use community off Weston Parkway in Cary. It had restaurants and shops, ice cream parlors, and hair salons. There was an apartment building behind the shops. I found the rental office and spoke to the woman there. Her name was Gina and she showed me two apartments, a two-bedroom and a one-bedroom. There was an outdoor pool for the community and a billiard table. It was a minute walk to Bonefish Grill and a Carolina Café. Gina told me they were intended to be sold as condos, but the real estate market crashed and the builders decided to turn them into rentals.

I told Gina that I needed the apartment for July 1. It was February. Gina said I should contact her around April 1. She would have a better idea about availability. I figured the two-bedroom apartment would be best. The apartment was small, but it would work. It was new and had an indoor storage unit as well.

The weather had improved everywhere. The kids had a two-week holiday from school because the school buses didn't have snow tires or snow plows. I left a message for Debbie on her cell. She rarely returned calls, but I wished Bob luck in his job search and told her I would be back soon.

I drove back to the hotel. I double-checked the weather on I-40 to the mountains and things were calm. I began to pack my clothes and paid my bill. I would return to the mountains in the morning. The move wouldn't be as expensive as an interstate move, but it was still a six-hour drive. I would worry about it later.

The highway was fine. I made it home in five hours. I managed not to get a speeding ticket. The mountains were white, and the sky was clear. Tomorrow, more snow was in the forecast for Asheville.

I went to the play readings once a month for enjoyment. I began organizing my box room, putting things that were not needed back into the boxes to make it easier as the moving time drew near.

I purchased a ticket to a Leonard Cohen concert. He became a Buddhist monk and took his vows of silence. The concert was good. He can't sing anymore but what a poet. I saw Dylan some years ago and he was dreadful. Again, I thought I was at Pritchard Park; the aroma of pot was everywhere... Leonard Cohen has a daughter; she had a child and the father is Rufus Wainwright, the singer. He is gay and has a lover and the baby is being brought up by I am not sure who. The Canadians were keeping the musical genes in the family.

There was an audition for the play *Shayna Maidel* by Rita Lebow. I rented the movie to perfect my Yiddish accent. I was asked by the director of the play to try out. I tried but apparently was not good enough. I was disappointed that I did not get a part. I went to the theater to watch the play. They did a phenomenal job as actors. The director did an outstanding job of directing, a labor of love.

Time travels slowly when you are having fun. I met someone at the library. We were looking at CDs. He was a hiker and a camper. We spoke, and he asked for my phone number. I told him I would be doing a lot of travelling—a white lie, half true. He did hand me a CD and said I might enjoy it. I thanked him and went to the check out with the CD of Abbey

Lincoln. She was a jazz vocalist who composed her own music. She was also an actress. I purchased the CD for my own collection.

I tried to enjoy the rest of my time in Asheville. Spring was in the air. Flowers were budding here and there—a sense of calm blanketed me. I had a plan, a destination. I tried to be patient and pack a little each day to make the move simpler in June.

I was in a state of limbo. I didn't date. I was tired of the dance. I was tired of men. I wanted time alone to gather my belongings and become more comfortable in being alone.

I discovered more wonderful restaurants downtown. I walked the cobblestone streets of Asheville. I began to say my goodbyes like I did in Westhampton and Sarasota. It was a silent journey to spots of beauty and memories.

It was moving day again. The movers would meet me in Cary tomorrow. They left with the stuff. I left with my box of words and a car full of valuables. I now owned an automatic, blow-up air mattress. I drove to Cary. I will sleep; I was prepared. The move-out was slow. The one mini- elevator in the building was a problem, but no more.

I said goodbye to the homeless men. I brought them boxes of Dunkin' Donuts and left.

My new theory was if the move-in goes well, then it will be a good stay. Also, if the nurses at a doctor's office are nice and kind, then chances are the doctor was good.

The drive was peaceful, and, again, I was excited and wondered about my nomadic tendencies. I listened to Abbey Lincoln on the trip. Her music was moody-choly.

I loved it. She drove me to Cary, or should I say we shared the drive? I parked the car and brought my personal belongings into the apartment. I had a shopping cart that was handy to load up. Numerous trips were made and the last cart trip was my state-of-the-art air mattress. I plugged it in, and it became a bed for me. I found the bed sheets and I went to Carolina Café for a sandwich. I planned on going to bed early—very early.

It was quiet, not a sound. There were bits and pieces of Asheville that I missed. It was a city, but I was feeling suburban at the moment. I was in Cary, and my sister-in-law Debbie lived close to me.

There was a resemblance between Ron and Debbie: She was named for Debbie Reynolds and Ron was named for Ronald Reagan, the third-rate actor and fourth-rate president, according to some. Their parents were born in Eastern Europe. Their father, Abraham, was born in Poland when the borders were changing and Ella, their mother, was born in Austria. Their parents met in England; they were members of a radical youth movement. They left Eastern Europe before the ghettos and camps. My mother-in-law believed she lost her three brothers and all of her family, but it was never documented. She never wanted to research it. Abe was in the English army. Ron was born in England; I have a picture of him and his parents coming to America on the Queen Elizabeth. He was three years old. In the black-and-white photograph, he had adorable blond curls with short, wool pants. His mother looked like Ingrid Bergman, and Abe resembled Gene Hackman. His mother had auburn hair and freckles.

Their plan was to move to Israel, Australia, or America. They did not speak English; they spoke German. Abe had a brother who was a doctor in the States. If you had a sponsor, you could gain entry into the U.S. I think they wanted to go to Israel but his brother sponsored them. I wondered what would have happened if had they gone to Israel instead. I would not have met Ron. I would not have the photo of the three of them on the boat and the life I have now. They left Europe; they left family behind that did not survive. They didn't know the language. I left home by choice; I left to seek my fate, change my fate. They went to

England, and avoided annihilation.

I waited for my furniture. It was promised for tomorrow. I was glad that my new residence was a simple trip from Asheville. I was hopeful that I would find a place to reside that suited me. I was aware of the good fortune I had in being able to choose my destination.

The move-in was fine with easy access to the apartment. Bonefish Grill was a minute walk from the new apartment. I fell asleep, fully clothed, with the lights on.

I remembered our first anniversary: I was working at the admissions office for the American Friends of Hebrew University on the upper east side of Manhattan. It was a program where students in the U.S. spend their junior year at the Hebrew University in Israel. I was within walking distance of Bloomingdale's. I bought Ron two Lacoste tennis shirts, navy and racing-car green, and white shorts. They were expensive but he loved his tennis clothes. He had a slight resemblance to John Newcomb, a tennis player from Australia.

When Ron's parents moved to America, they lived in Queens, New York. Ella, his mother, was a seamstress and Abraham found work at Franklin Simon, a department store for women in Manhattan, as a bookkeeper. It later evolved into his working on their giant-sized computer.

His parents discovered state parks. They played tennis at Bethpage State Park on Long Island. Ron's love and lust for tennis was born there. Ron's friends from elementary school, junior high school, and Forest Hills High School were all bitten by the tennis bug. I had to compete with the friends for time with Ron. His friends' parents were American-born.

He convinced his mother to enroll in evening English classes at the high school. Ron believed his father was a spy or double-agent because of the German accent. They spoke German at home; Ron understood all of it but spoke none of it.

He looked handsome in his Lacoste tennis apparel. His moustache was a tad red and brown, his sideburns were brown and auburn. He was five feet eleven, and I was five feet two. I had long, brown hair down my back and dark, chocolate-brown eyes. Whenever Van Morrison's "Brown Eyed Girl" played on the radio, he said it was our song. When I hear it now, I smile—so long ago, it feels like yesterday.

Our passports from 1971 reflect a bearded, long-haired Ron and a Mona Lisa version of me. He looked like a draft dodger and he was in a way. He had asthma as a kid. His Uncle Moritz sponsored his family in gaining entrance to America. As Ron's draft number was getting closer, he would run around the block numerous times and have an asthma attack. He would then go to the doctor and have it documented. There were times when he did the run and visited his uncle's medical office. It was a success; the draft board was uninterested in Ron serving his country. They never realized that one of the doctors had the same last name as Ron.

There was something about Cary that felt right. I was sixty-two. I felt good, I was relatively healthy. I saw signs for an adult retirement community in western Cary. It was called Carolina Preserve. My GPS was not updated enough; it was a new community for active seniors. The GPS managed to get me lost, and I ended up in Durham. My GPS and I found the community after a few wrong turns.

There was a large clubhouse, fitness center, indoor lap pool, and fitness classes. I viewed the seven or eight models. They had villas, but they were small. I didn't want to share walls with anyone. I found a model that I liked. I spoke with the Pulte saleswoman and the pricing was changing, in addition, I didn't understand some of the figures that she came up with. The homes could be competed in six months. The winters were mild here, most of the time.

Debbie and Bob visited me in the new apartment and Bob hooked up my computer. The second bedroom in the apartment became the computer/storage room.

I went on Match.moron for one last time. It was a time-consuming pastime and unproductive, to say the least. I was writing to a man who lost his wife recently. We met for lunch at a Chinese restaurant. He was a scientist with a doctorate in molecular biology. He was working part time at the Environmental Protection Agency. He was shy, sweet, and from North Dakota. After we met for lunch, he asked if he could hug me and I said yes. It was innocent and pure. We went out again. His name was Dan.

I returned to Carolina Preserve to look again at the development. I was finally feeling like I might be close to having a home built. I loved that it was new, and I could choose what I wanted in the house. The economy was bad; it was a good time to buy. I was ripe, I traveled to many places and was tired of the nomadic life.

I went out with Dan again; he had tickets to the Carolina Ballet. I took ballet as a young girl. I took modern dance in high school and danced in many school performances. I was never able to convince Ron to go to the ballet. Dan and I also attended the symphony. I enjoyed his company but he wanted to get married, not to me yet, but it was important to him. We saw each other on the weekends. We took a trip to Asheville for four days in the fall.

I liked Cary and Dan; life was good. Cary reminded me of New York. The mountains were four hours away; the beaches were about two or three hours away. Life was less hectic; people were kind. I brought Debbie and Bob out to view the community. They thought the people looked old and some were, but I was sixty-two and ready. There were other widows and divorced women.

The negotiations on the house were going poorly. I realized I needed an outside broker to work on my behalf. I hired a woman who sold properties at the preserve.

I decided which model I wanted. I was offered a loft. The second floor had an enormous living room and bedroom with a full bath. This would be perfect for Adam and the children he might not have.

I had a contract on a home. I would await the building and birth of my home. Pulte said it should be ready in six months. I had a six-month lease.

Dan called; I told him I had a contract on the house. I asked him if he wanted to see the community. He was willing to take a ride. Dan lived in Raleigh in a large house. He had lived there for thirty-two years or so. He picked me up and we got lost. We found it and I showed him the model.

He liked the model and its layout. He didn't care for the concept of community living with a homeowner association. He was not fond of restrictions on the color of the front door. I wanted to show him around. I liked the plan and Dan. His home was situated on two acres. It had a pond, deer, and shade trees. I was excited about my house.

We spent most of our weekends together; Dan suggested that he bring clothes to my apartment. I thought it was a fine idea. He brought some clothing for the weekends.

His wife had died painfully and quickly. She was diagnosed with pancreatic cancer. I spent Thanksgiving of 2010 at Dan's home in Raleigh with his son, daughter-in-law, and granddaughter. It was a nice day. I received invitations to Thanksgiving through the years, but I never accepted an invitation. Mostly, I continued the tradition Ron and I had of getting Chinese food on Christmas and Thanksgiving but not that year.

The holiday season was in full bloom. My house was almost completed. I boxed most of my things: much of it was packed in the apartment's storage unit.

11
THE DAY I KIDNAPPED DADDIO

M y father was ninety years old, residing in Ft. Lauderdale. My first word in this life was Irvie. His name was Irving. He called me at odd hours, complaining of not feeling well. He was an active octogenarian with a girlfriend. I assumed he would live forever. His father lived to be ninety-seven.

His mantra was "I feel sick."

"Where do you hurt, Dad?"

"I don't remember; I can't play cards." I heard the sadness in his voice. He was lost. He was a card player—a good one.

Ellen flew to Florida to visit with him. His living room was overflowing with clothes. He had been ironing his shirts on the dining-room table as he had done years before. He told Ellen that there were toxins in the apartment. They were the cause of his maladies.

Ellen hired a cleaning service to iron his shirts and clean the apartment. He was satisfied and Ellen flew back home. We had hoped he was missing family, and a visit would sustain him. My plan was to see him after I closed on the house. My closing was set for December 28, 2010. It rarely snows in Raleigh. There was a snowstorm on Christmas Day. I spent the holidays with Dan's family. I slept at Dan's house; his driveway was covered in ice and snow. I was driving a Mustang. I was trapped indoors.

The gray sky was pebbled with a snow quilt of white, silent hush. The birds and critters' footprints created a design worthy of an etching. My cell phone broke the peace. I picked up the phone.

"Marsha, how are you; where are you?"

"Dad, I'm OK. What about you?"

"It's the toxins; there's mold here and I have to leave."

"Dad, I'll be in Florida as soon as I can, I promise."

Kidnapped Daddio

183

My closing was scheduled in two days. The snowstorm did not delay the closing, but the closing took four hours. The paperwork was delayed, but I was a homeowner. I returned to the apartment, and the movers arrived as I was getting out of the car. They moved me into the house in record time. The trip was maybe eight miles from door to door. My boxes were lined up in the garage and sun room in absolutely no order. Chaos prevailed; I worked out of chaos.

I called Dan and told him I was flying to Florida to see my father. He said he wanted to come with me. I wondered why. I said, "No, it was okay." He insisted on being there with me. I relented and said OK. If I didn't realize what a kind man he was before, I certainly knew it now. I made airline reservations for us. We flew to Ft. Lauderdale early the next morning. We were at my father's apartment by ten a.m. I had the keys to his place, but I didn't want to alarm him by walking in.

I knocked on the door, no answer. I called him on my cell phone, nothing. I went to the parking lot to see if his car was there. I knew his spot, and the car was gone. I figured that was a good sign; he was out and about. I entered his apartment to find his clothes clinging to the dining room chairs. The couch cradled his shirts and slacks, and his shoes were in the kitchen, of course.

I found many anti-mold applications scattered about:

    1) Mold bomb beware

    2) Hydrogen peroxide

    3) Tea tree oil

    4) Grapefruit seed extract

    5) Vinegar

    6) Baking soda

    7) Mold BeGone

    8) Toxic No More

    9) Bye Bye Mold

His apartment had a thick odor of toxicity emanating from the spray can fumes. Those chemicals could make him sick. I decided to wait outside for him. I called his cell phone number. He picked up.

"Hi, Dad, where are you?"

"It's bad."

"I'll see you in a few minutes." He acquiesced.

I was waiting for him in the parking lot of his condo. Dan was with me, and it was a good feeling. It was comforting to have someone share in my family calamities. I was used to handling my major and minor crises solo. I saw my father driving in to park the car. I walked over to his parking spot and greeted him. I introduced him to Dan. My father smelled like gasoline; his gas tank was opened. He told me about the mold and that he was dying of mold disease.

"Marsh, I have been poisoned, I am toxic." Well, I knew that, I lived with him.

"What happened at the gas station, Dad?"

"They didn't have the right gas and this looks like my car, but it is a phony car."

"Let's go into the apartment." I asked my father if he wanted to take a shower since he smelled like a trucker. Diesel Daddy did not want a shower.

He looked too thin, and I had the sense that he was not eating. My father was an anorexic octogenarian. I went food shopping while Dan stayed with him. He gave me the keys to the car, and I bought the basics; there was nothing in the fridge. I supposed he was on the anti-mold spray and gasoline diet.

I made egg salad for lunch. We ate in the small kitchen. The dining room table was laden with his clothes. I supposed his closet was empty. I didn't look. He looked at the egg salad and told me the eggs were not cooked. He threw the egg salad in the trash. He began screaming at me.

He was ranting about the eggs being uncooked. He was slamming and kicking the doors. Dan was outside making a phone call. My father would not slam the doors if Dan was in the house. I was becoming concerned about his blood pressure and mine. I didn't want Dan to see him like this. A wave of nausea was moments away. It had been a long time since I was around this piece of my father.

I remembered as a kid seeing my father huddled in his old army blanket. I asked my mother what was wrong with him, and she told me he had the flu. He was moaning and rocking, back and forth, on the rocking chair. I believed her. She would never lie to me.

When I was a kid living in the housing project in Long Island City, I wanted to take my green baby carriage out for a walk. Be Nice said it was too hot and that the carriage might melt. I didn't want my babies to melt. We would have to put the carriage in the elevator, and it probably was a hot day. I knew that Be Nice told white lies. A white lie, she told me, was a harmless lie that was meant to not hurt another's feelings. I created a poncho of sorts out of that army blanket in my bohemian era.

Dan thought I should take my father to the doctor. I called his general practitioner who was a DO, a doctor of osteopathic medicine. He put up quite a fight, my father. He was pacing up and down the condo. Dr. Orman told me I could bring him in. He wouldn't let me drive. He wanted Dan to drive. We had the address and arrived moments later.

Dr. Orman was in his fifties. He shook my father's hand and said, "Irv, you smell like gasoline." My father said nothing.

I introduced myself to Dr. Orman who looked at me. I told him a bit about my father's behavior, and we spoke of him in the third person which saddened and disturbed me. I suggested to Dr. Orman that perhaps I would hire someone to stay with him and cook for him for five hours each day. Dr. Orman looked at me and said my father was in no condition to live on his own and make decisions. I want you to take him to the psychiatric ward connected to the hospital in the next building from this one. My father was expressionless; he was unresponsive. Dr. Orman decided to Baker Act my father, which meant an involuntary commitment to the psychiatric ward for observation by trained professionals for seventy-two hours.

He was passive and old, but he played in tennis tournaments when he was eighty years old. He lifted weights and had no body fat. He was small, five feet nothing, with a large will to excel and he did. He played golf and had a hole in one. He was a doer and stranger to me. Ron and my father got along. They both loved their sports. Ron loved me and I loved him.

Two hours later, my father was admitted to the psychiatric hospital. Dan and I drove back to my father's condo in silence. I was embarrassed that Dan witnessed my father's undoing, but if he was upset he never showed it. Another man would have said to call me when it's over with your father. Dan said he signed on for better or for worse. He rubbed my back in the condo, and I fell asleep on the couch.

I was never in my father's condo without one of my parents in the house. Be Nice, my mother, died three months before Ron. I was off balance, adrift, dreary, and hungry. Tears dripped down my cheeks, the salty tears helped me think clearly. It wiped the slate; my eyes ached to see Ron. I didn't want Dan to see me crying. He might begin to cry and then what? He was a new widower.

We went out to eat. Dan had never been in Florida. I brought him to a Jewish-style restaurant. Ft. Lauderdale was the east coast, the New York, New Jersey coast. I thought I would shock the Dakotas out of him. He took it in stride.

Dan asked me to marry him. This was the second time he asked. The first time I told him he shouldn't be dating since he was newly widowed. He laughed and ignored me completely. This time, I was grateful for his being with me through this ordeal. I almost said yes. I said maybe. Do you marry a man because he was amazingly kind to the father you disliked? I married Ron because Be Nice Bernice, my mother, loved him.

We were back at the condo. We slept in the king-sized bed. Dan fell asleep in an instant.

I took a Klonopin; my mind was still racing. I remembered that my father had a suitcase filled with documents from the Veteran's Administration.

I found the suitcase in a corner of his closet near his shoes. I dragged it into the living room. I left the snoring Dan alone; he never knew I left. There were documents from the Veteran's Administration from 1942 when he entered the army. He was a radio operator in the army. There were pounds of pages of medical records. His military service was from August 1942 to February 1945. He was honorably discharged due to psychoneurosis. In 2013, it was called depressive neurosis. He was morbidly depressed, anxious, and delusional.

My father believed he was dying in 1945 and held on to that belief until he died at ninety-one. He was obsessed with losing his mind. When he was in the psychiatric ward in Florida, he told a nurse in a semi-whisper that he was poisoned and frightened that others would catch it and they would put him into a mental institution like his mother and he would die there as his mother did. The nurse reassured him that was not going to happen. He stopped eating and no longer cared about how he looked. He was living in his depressed head.

I organized the information. I separated the VA records from his private doctor records. Most of the records were from the VA. I read and re-read the same phrases over and over again: neurosis, anxiety, depression, dementia, anger, and mentally disturbed. I was tired but sleep was not in my future. There were notes from his internist that they discovered a mass in one of his kidneys; the other kidney had lesions.

The kidney with the large mass was the kidney with 65 percent function. My father never told me about his medical issues. His girlfriend disappeared at the first sign of illness; some of his money disappeared as well.

Why did I organize the records? Would it change my father's mental state? My father needed to live in an assisted-living facility. He required 'around the clock' care.

An intervention was in order. I assigned Dan to pack my father's clothes. I showed him where the suitcases were, and he meticulously folded his shirts and underwear, army style. The slacks and shirts were placed in suitcases as well. I packed his medications and papers from the VA and current medical reports. Most of his clothes were in the car in the trunk.

The psychiatric hospital officially told me that my father had to be admitted to a senior care center in three days. They were done with him. They added more anti-psychotic medication, and he was given his walking papers.

I decided quickly that I would bring him to North Carolina. Dan knew of a facility, but they did not have any rooms available. They recommended one of their sister communities. It was an independent-living facility. My father was accepted there. He was not independent but I agreed. If I admitted him to a facility in Florida, no one would be visiting him. I had to be there for him. He was my father.

I made airline reservations to Raleigh, North Carolina, for the three of us. I called a car service that picked us up at my father's condo. We transferred his clothes from the car to the trunk of the cab, and I told the driver the plan. He would drive us to the hospital and from the hospital we were going directly to the airport. We arrived at the hospital, and I proceeded to deceive my father for his own good as he had done for me years ago.

My father was dressed and ready to go. He insisted on going back to his apartment. I ignored him. The nurse put him in a wheelchair, and I crossed my fingers and prayed I could pull this off. We placed him in the cab. Dan and I acted as bookends with my father in the middle in case he tried to escape.

My father looked fragile and cute with his denim jacket and baseball cap. He looked at the windshield of the cab and told the driver this was not the route to his condo. *Oh, shit, now he's alert and sharp.* I told the driver that the sun was bothering my eyes; could he please lower the sun visors? He adjusted the sun visors to limit my father's view.

My father was agitated. "Sir, this is not the way to Tamarac."

The driver said there was road construction, and we would be taking a short cut. Great, he is now an accomplice to a kidnapping. My father looked tired, his eyes were closing, and he was nodding off. It seemed as if the medication they had given him at the hospital was finally kicking in. We arrived at the airport. Dan checked the luggage. I stayed with my father. He refused a wheelchair but he was calm and said nothing about his condo or his car.

The plane ride was less than two hours, and he slept most of the ride, like an infant from the motion and the humming of the plane. When I was in the car with my father, he would snap his fingers, hum, and whistle. I told him if he hums; he can't whistle. He told me that Be Nice Bernice, said the same thing. There were times when I would turn the music off. He no longer hummed or whistled. It was necessary to limit some of his OCD tendencies.

I wished Ron was here with me. He was my father, my charge, and my responsibility. I had been responsible for only Adam and myself for eight years; I wondered what this experience would be like... I was a caregiver again.

Debbie, Ron's sister, picked us up at the airport in Raleigh-Durham.

She drove us to Bel-Air, the independent-living facility. It was located on Creedmoor Road in Raleigh, about thirty minutes from my house. There was a mental institution that went by the name of Creedmoor in New York City. My father was passive, exhausted, and confused. I knew it was difficult to uproot a person, especially an elderly person, specifically your own father. I had no siblings to consult with though Ellen and I spoke all the time. I ultimately made the decision.

It was early afternoon, and they greeted us warmly. They showed us to my father's one-bedroom apartment. It was furnished modestly. I had taken his checkbook with me when we left his condo. I had to pay two months in advance. He didn't have enough money, so I gave them a check from my account. An aide asked my father if he was hungry. He was unresponsive. The trip and meds must have exhausted him. He never looked his age. He looked weary. I was amazed at how well-behaved he was.

I began to unpack his clothing. I hung the shirts and slacks in the closet. Dan made good choices for my father's clothes. I placed his shoes in the closet and put his underwear in the dresser. My father sat on the bed, way too tired to be difficult or demented.

My father was small, helpless, old, and confused. I wondered if I had made the right choice. I knew it was the only choice. I did the right thing. They helped him into his pajamas. I kissed him goodnight and told him I would see him in the morning.

I was back at my house in Cary with boxes everywhere. I slept in the guest room. I brought the one bed from Asheville and set it up in the small bedroom. My plan was to buy myself a new bedroom set but that would have to wait.

The one thing we forgot to bring from Florida was my father's cell phone. I called the facility to find out if he was sleeping. They said yes. I tossed and turned all night. His green-brown eyes separated from sanity while diving into pools of delusion. He saw bugs on the carpet. He saw large dogs moving on the fabrics and couches.

It was dark when I went to Bel-Air to visit my father. I took a shower and drank a cup of tea. The drive was thirty minutes with not much traffic. I remembered my grandmother when she mentally declined. One day, she put the red fruit bowl on her head and smiled at me. Soon after that, Be Nice Bernice visited with my grandmother in the nursing home in Queens, N.Y. I spent years overseeing Ron's care. I spent time with Be Nice when she was dying and Ron was critically ill. I made arrangements for friends to be with Ron when I visited with my mother.

I had conversations with my father after we were widowed; he was eighty-three when he met a woman. He said he wanted just ten more years of life. I thought he was a greedy old man. I wondered how he could say that to me. I was a grown woman, yet my father could hurt and anger me. I was the good wife, the good daughter.

When my time comes, I will go to Oregon, invite my nearest and dearest and have a party—a suicide party. Suicide is legal in Oregon; there is a pill. I will party, dance, and die.

DAY ONE IN ASSISTED LIVING...

It was eight-fifteen a.m. and residents were walking on their own; some had walkers. It was time for breakfast. I went to my father's room. He was sleeping soundly in a chair. I didn't dare wake him. I remembered when Adam was a baby; I was quiet when he slept. I enjoyed the peacefulness of having time alone. Today would be the day when he really lets me have it, I thought. I went downstairs to the lobby. I found the evening nurse who was on her way home. She told me my father slept well.

When it was nine a.m., I came back to his room. He sat in the chair near his bed. Once he saw me, it began.

He asked me, "Where am I? Where is my car? I need my car, Marsha."

"Dad, we're in North Carolina," I replied.

"Marsha, you live here. I want to live in your house." The good daughter was speechless. She smiled and pretended she didn't hear a word. Oftentimes, silence is the only correct answer. "Let's go to your house."

I thought back to the old Rosemary Clooney song, "Come on-a my house, my house I'm gonna give you candy."

"Dad, would you like some coffee?"

"Yes," he said. Coffee became the equalizer, the peacemaker, wampum, trinkets. The closet was filled with much of his clothing.

"Marsha, I need clothes, take me shopping." The stores were not open yet. I suggested he eat breakfast, and he said, "Only if you do, Marsh." I didn't want breakfast, but I was well-behaved and sat at a table with him. He drank four cups of coffee. I can't imagine who will not be sleeping this evening.

At ten a.m. he was dressed and raring to go shopping. He insisted that the clothes in the closet were poisoned though only he could see the toxins. He advised me to throw away all of his clothing. He was capable of walking on his own. We were on our way to Macy's. He liked my car. He wanted to drive it. I wanted to let him, as long as I was not in the car. A part of him knew he couldn't drive, but he was big on denial and very active until six months ago.

He was ninety and looked like a man in his seventies. It was a blessing and a curse. Once we were in Macy's, we headed to the men's department. He was looking at Tommy Hilfiger shirts and Dockers slacks. I found a salesman, not an easy task these days: shortage of help, intentional cutbacks in the sales staff. He measured my father from head to toe. My father was five feet. I wasn't able to go in the dressing room, so the salesman was wonderful. He went in the dressing room with him. The slacks fit; we purchased three pairs of slacks and four shirts that looked exactly like those that were in the closet at Bel-Air.

We returned in time for lunch. I planned to bring him to the dining room and then I would remove the clothes from his closet and have them cleaned and pressed. He refused to eat unless I ate with him. I wondered how he was able to manipulate me in his diminished state. I sat at the table and ordered food for him and me. I went to the salad bar and picked up a salad for him. He gave me his order. I was his personal waitress. I was nauseous. He ate his salad, even though I put the wrong dressing on it. He ate the chicken and four more cups of coffee and strawberry ice cream. I had a three-course meal at lunch. I will gain two pounds, and he will tell me I am fat.

I kissed him goodbye, went to his room, and took the shirts to the cleaners. I arrived at my new house. Instead of a box room, I inhabited a box house. I lived in my cozy guest bedroom. It had the furniture that was in the guest bedroom in Westhampton. It was the room Ron slept in after his dialysis treatments, and it was the room Adam slept in when he visited us. I told Dan that the owners of my house had not given me permission to move into the master bedroom. It didn't feel like it was my home since I had resided in other people's houses for so many years. I planned to visit my father for an hour tomorrow and then have the rest of the day for me.

There was a load of paperwork to take care of for my father. He had a long-term care policy. I needed to contact the insurance company and file a claim. I was on hold for over forty-five minutes. I refused to be discouraged; I napped intermittently. I spoke with them for half an hour. They mailed an application form to my house. My father's policy was for one hundred ten dollars a night for a total of three years. It would be about three thousand dollars a month, depending on how many days in the month.

Dan was a blessing: I was enormously fortunate to have him in my life. Dan was working part time. He came to my house on Fridays or Saturday mornings through Sunday. We had tickets to the ballet once a month on

Saturday night. We had tickets to the symphony and would get tickets to any show we wanted. We saw *Cirque Du Soleil*. On Sundays, we woke early; I made breakfast for us. He went to church early. He met his son and granddaughter there. I visited with my father.

Dan and I tried to go to Carrboro for the day. We would get in the car and go. We would be an hour from Bel-Air, and the nurse called to let me know my father took a tumble. Dan and I returned to Bel-Air. They had taken him to the hospital for observation. Dan dropped me off at the hospital. I felt awful about ruining our weekend.

I found my father in the ER. He felt secure in the hospital. They took fine care of him. They x-rayed his elbow. We would wait for the results.

"What happened, Dad?"

"I don't know." I noticed his slippers in the corner of the room. He wore his slippers instead of shoes. I decided I would take him shopping for orthopedic shoes that had support. I waited for over two hours until the x-ray was read. He was shook up but not in terrible pain. He was cranky.

"Marsh, get me out of here now," he demanded.

I went to the nurses' station to get food for him. They promised to deliver a cheese sandwich. I was a pro at this, unfortunately. They returned with a sandwich and a doctor. The good news was nothing was broken, just a bad bruise, and the bad news was the sandwich was not real cheese, according to my father. The food in North Carolina was not real food, so he threw it on the floor and had a tantrum.

"I want my car now, Marsha, or buy me a new car today!" He had quite a way of diminishing me and making me feel insecure and worthless. I hated feeling like that. I hadn't experienced that in a long time. I knew he was frustrated, suffering, and ill, but I didn't want to suffer. He saved the nastiness for me.

The ambulance brought us back to Bel-Air. Dan left with his car. He would pick me up later at Bel-Air. I knew that people who are cared for treat the people closest to them poorly. Through all of his ailments, Ronnie never demeaned me. Occasionally, he was short with a nurse or roommate.

Dan called me on my cell phone and came to Bel-Air within half an hour. We made sure my father was comfortable and left. It must have been dinnertime. We went out to eat. I was tired, and Dan came back to my house. I thanked him for his kindness. My father liked Dan.

The first time they met, my father asked Dan where he was born. He said North Dakota. Dan asked if my father was ever there. My father said, "No, why would I?" It was a born-and-bred New Yorker reply.

I was glad to be home. Dan and I watched a movie. We went to bed. I listened to him snore. We woke up early and made love. Dan went to church; I visited with my father.

My father was a handful. I never knew what mood he'd display for me when I showed up to visit him. The nurses and aides loved him; he was charming. He flirted with the prettiest members of the staff. He denied that he was settling in. I purchased a cell phone for him. He needed contact, and I needed to be able to contact him. I should have known that his sense of time was non-existent. He awoke early and called me at three-thirty a.m. He was waiting for me to take him clothes shopping. He had a wardrobe that many men would envy.

We graduated from clothes to snacks, cookies, and candy. We would go out to lunch. Sometimes, Dan came with us. My father, after numerous falls, graduated to a walker that he would drag behind him in the grocery store. The goodies that we bought in the store he would give away to the residents in the evening.

One day when I arrived at his apartment, he was naked except for his diaper. He placed all of his clothes in trash bags. "Marsha, I have nothing to wear and I want to go home to Florida, get me a car." Luckily, I had many of his clothes dry cleaned and they were with me. I showed him the freshly ironed shirts and slacks. He began to get dressed but still wanted to go shopping for more. Today, he wanted bargains, so I dragged him to T.J. Maxx. He trailed behind me with his walker, if I did nothing else, I tired him out. "Marsh, bring the car around." I found a weary, old man, waiting to be chauffeured back to the facility, his new home.

They had doctors who visited the residents. I made an appointment with one of the geriatric doctors. I contacted the VA in Durham, and they suggested that he have an appointment with a geriatric psychiatrist. Durham was twenty miles away from Bel-Air, but I made the visit early in the morning so we didn't get stuck in five p.m. traffic. If you go to the VA, the visits and medications are free. Once you're in the system, they mail three months' worth of meds. We spoke with a young woman doctor who had my father perform some memory tests. He was charming and appropriate. He discussed his anxiety related to the poisons. I told the doctor it was a recurrent theme. She described it as a hallucination. She added new anti-psychotic medication to the regimen. He was ingesting twenty-five pills a day. Ron had the indoor record.

My father required aides at night to get him ready for bed and stay with him through the night. He would awake and worry about dying. They dressed him in the morning and brought him to breakfast. I suppose that when you were ninety, you give thought to dying. I think about dying. What would happen if I passed before my father?

One evening he fell and hit his head on the couch in the lobby and bled on the carpet. He was taken to the emergency room later that evening.

At midnight, after I was called, I dressed and headed to the hospital. It was a thirty-minute ride—no one was on the road to Raleigh. Cary is a sleepy city. My father was having an MRI or CAT scan of his brain. I waited for him to return to the ER. The CAT scan and MRI showed no abnormalities. He was whisked off in two hours to Bel-Air. I stayed with him. I drove back to his apartment when the ambulance came for him. The night nurse helped him to bed.

"Good night, Dad," and he was asleep before I said good night.

I drove home, just me and an occasional deer. It was four a.m. and I was home by four-twenty a.m. I went to bed and dreamed about unpacking. I was doomed to be surrounded by boxes for eternity.

At about eight a.m., my father wanted to know where I was. I was sleeping; we had a late night last night. He remembered nothing.

"Dad, I have a cold. I will visit with you tomorrow." It was a white lie. I didn't have a cold yet; I figured I would visit him the following day.

One of the head nurses suggested my father be put on hospice. The people from hospice came to visit and assessed him. They decided based on age and the kidney cancer he was a good candidate. Ron was on hospice for three days. I joined a bereavement group after Ron died. I became a volunteer for hospice in New York. An older gentleman visited with my father, and my father told him not to come back. My father fired a volunteer. They should have sent a woman to him. A social worker came; my father was well cared for. He was busy, and I tried to visit less.

We celebrated his birthday on June 27 at my house. Adam was there, as well as Ellen and her children: Randy, Lisa, Alexander, Katherine, and Jason. Debbie, Ron's sister, and her daughter Jennifer attended. Dan's children and granddaughter were there. I made everyone wear birthday hats. We had Italian food, wings, and pizza. We had birthday cake and ninety-one candles. My father convinced himself that he would be moving into my house. In the car on the way to the party, he was telling Dan and me how he made tilapia. He breaded the fish and then baked it in the oven.

Everything my father said I acted out like I was playing crazy charades, so I pantomimed the baking of the tilapia down to the bread crumbs. I was laughing at my private joke. He seemed happy. My father was beginning to fade. Dan and I drove him back to Bel-Air. He never mentioned the move-in.

The hospice people were extraordinary. They bathed him three times a week. They talked to him about his feelings. They encouraged him to participate in some of the activities at the facility which my father was not interested in. A social worker visited twice a month.

It was a lifesaver for me. I made a donation to Wake Hospice in gratitude for the care they gave my father and the respite I had. He didn't admit to having pain, but he grimaced a lot. He was old and sick.

My father graduated from hospice. He was no longer hospice eligible since he was not declining. After six months on hospice, he was re-evaluated and discharged. He didn't understand what it meant. I knew he would miss the kind people like his main nurse, Donna.

Dan wanted to get married before something happened to my father. He wasn't pressuring me, but I felt the pressure. My father was, of course, at my marriage to Ron. I would not be a good wife for Dan or anyone. I treasured my independence.

My father had many lives. He fell again on his arm and was transferred to the ER while Dan and I were walking for a cure for Alzheimer's. Dan drove me home so I could get my car. I was wearing leggings and sneakers for the walk. We had ballet tickets for this evening, and it didn't look like I was going to be in attendance. I told Dan to call me, but I figured he might as well go to the ballet without me.

I loved ballet; I loved getting dressed up for the occasion. My father had a contusion. It was bandaged and taped, so back to Bel-Air he went. Dan called and said he would pick me up. I was not dressed. I was stinky and sweaty from the walk. He picked me up anyway, and we went to the ballet. Dan was wearing slacks and a sport jacket with a tie. I looked like a slob, but I was elated to be away from facilities, hospitals, and, specifically, my father. The ballet was therapeutic and mesmerizing. I was transported to another land of colors, music, unfamiliar leaping, flying pointed toes, stunning costumes, and dancing with abandon and control.

I remembered visiting my father in Florida nine months after Ron died. He wanted me to meet his pool table buddies. He wanted me to look good. He wanted me to get dressed up and wear lots of makeup, so they would think what a lucky guy he was to have such a beautiful daughter. The men were in their eighties with their shorts belted high above their waists. I complied and was pissed. I thought I did that as a kid. When we left to meet his friends, my father whistled at me. Why did I still visit him?

I was trying to understand how my looking good helped his ego. He put makeup on my mother and polished her nails when she was ill and confused. I supposed order out of chaos. If you looked good, all was right. My father took care of his mother when she was mentally ill. He had to leave high school. He was bright, but his father commanded him to be the caregiver.

We drove home from the ballet. I told Dan how grateful I was to be at the ballet with him. The next ballet performance, I will be dressed to the nines.

My father was no longer on hospice; he needed his walker all the time. His balance was not great. He did not eat much. They had his food chopped or pureed. He didn't sleep much. They had him cut down on his coffee intake. I brought him milk shakes when I visited. He drank them quickly to the last drop. I visited but didn't stay very long. He was taking four different anti-depressants and anti-psychotic pills but was perpetually depressed. He was tired, cranky, and old. The milk shakes gave him a momentary lift.

I was sleeping; I heard the phone ringing. I figured it was another hallucination or an imaginary phone call or dream. I opened my eyes and, indeed, the phone was ringing. My father fell again. They were bringing him to the emergency room. It was two-thirty a.m. I drove to the hospital; he was being x-rayed. He was riddled with pain. The doctor told me he broke six ribs.

"Dad, you are like a cat."

"Let me die," he murmured. This was his first fracture. There was nothing the doctors could do for broken ribs, other than giving him pain medicine.

"Dad, the ribs will heal on their own. You are an amazing healer." The doctors were forever telling us that.

He looked fragile and helpless. The helplessness was the worst part of it all. He was admitted to the hospital. We were waiting for an available room. I stayed with him through his moans and groans. Pain is a small word with enormous meaning. I held his hand, but he was annoyed by my touch. He was annoyed that he broke something. I didn't ask him how it happened. There was no advantage in knowing.

They transferred him from the ER to the geriatric floor. He had a private room for now. The nurses came in to assess him. I traveled with a list of his medications. They put an IV of fluids in his veiny veins. They asked him to breathe in and out. He did and was close to screaming out from the pain of it all. They put an IV of antibiotics in his vein. He was hooked up and getting sleepy. The doctor came in to check on him. He told me that when an elderly patient breaks a rib not only does it heal slowly, but there was a risk of pneumonia. He was on antibiotics. My father was resting and sleeping. He had a long night.

I stayed until morning. They brought him breakfast which he refused to eat. *When I return, I will get him a milk shake,* I thought.

"Dad, how bad is the pain?" He grimaced; I tried to find a nurse to see what the orders were for pain pills. Within twenty minutes, a nurse gave him all of his regular pills and a pain pill. I kissed him goodbye and told him I loved him and would be back later. He should rest now.

I drove home and fell asleep, fully dressed. I heard the phone ring. It was in my dream. I woke up at two p.m. I called the hospital to check on him. They said he had a small lunch. I showered quickly and left the house. I bought a milk shake for him. He sipped it up in seven seconds. He looked flushed. I found a nurse; he had a fever. They added another pill to his bag of drugs. A young, beautiful Asian doctor walked in and expressed her concern about his fever and malaise. My father perked up; he was preparing to flirt with her. He told her she was beautiful, and she told him he had a fever.

She was adding another antibiotic to the IV. They might give him a chest x-ray today. When he coughed, the pain was unbearable. He might break another rib. I stayed until he had a small dinner. He thanked me for coming. I was shocked. I kissed him goodbye and told him I would visit him tomorrow.

I arrived early the next day. Dr. Chu was making early rounds. She didn't like that he still had a fever. I saw a priest walk into my father's room to visit with my father. I wondered why he was there. My father was friendly and enjoyed the visit. I found Dr. Chu and asked her why the priest came to see my father. She felt that my father might want to speak with a holy man. His fever was rising; he had pneumonia now. "Pneumonia is the old man's friend." I have heard that once before. Pneumonia can be a kinder end than other organ breakdowns. My father will beat this. It doesn't matter if a priest, rabbi, or the Dalai Lama appeared. He wasn't ready. I called Adam and Ellen to tell them, and they were concerned. I would stay in touch. I gave them his phone number in the hospital.

It was touch and go. The fever broke. His color was better. He would stay in the hospital a few more days. He was tough, old Daddio. Dr. Chu returned to see him; she was pleased and shocked. I told her never to underestimate anything. My father dodged another one.

The social worker came to speak to us about the next plan. Daddio required physical therapy. He was improving, but he was not mobile. The broken ribs weakened his body. He needed to go to a rehabilitation facility. He thought he was going to march on out of there with his walker, but that was not the case. The social worker recommended three places. I looked at them and chose the one that seemed the best. None of these places were appealing. There were some younger people with serious injuries, but the majority of the population was old and disabled. I hoped I made the right choice.

I asked the social worker to visit with my father to explain the plan to him. She was pretty, and it would be an opportunity for him to flirt and swallow the bitter medicine. Again, I was packing clothes, hauling them into the car. I drove to the rehab facility without my father. I set his clothes up in the closets and drawers. I met his roommate who was watching me place my father's clothes in the closet. I introduced myself and told his roommate, Tom, that my father would be arriving later today. The roommate, Tom, laughed when he saw all of my father's clothes.

"Where does your father think he's going? Does he have a job?" I laughed too. I suppose my father's job was staying alive and needling me. I drove back to the hospital to bring him to the rehab place.

He was nervous. He was placed in a wheelchair, and they put him in my car with much difficulty. He thought he was going back to the apartment, even though he was told numerous times that he was on his way to rehab. I asked him if he remembered when Be Nice was in rehab. A frightened look stirred in his eyes. I sensed that he was losing vocabulary, the meaning of things. I wanted to tell him there was no meaning, that life was random and chronic, but I held myself back because it might not be the truth. Daddio would not know what I was talking about, and I was as confused and empty as his eyes.

Another move-in, another day in paradise. I knew the room number since I placed his belongings there. A large, loud unattractive nurse introduced herself to us. Even though his eyes were failing, his eyes were offended. Her tone of voice was abrasive. Was this Dante's *Inferno?* She was gruff; she yelled at patients. She was the head nurse and why she went into the caring profession was beyond comprehension.

My father was assessed again by the physical therapy department. He needed to have strength restored in his arms to enable him to rise out of the wheelchair independently. A schedule was set up for three days a week of exercises. He wasn't eating at all. I brought him milkshakes; he drank it, eating little else.

I watched him as he sat in the wheelchair like a prisoner planning the next move, scraping or chiseling a spoon to become a weapon. He sat in the chair with his hands on the armrest. I gazed at him as he attempted to raise himself out of the chair. He went to therapy and after each session, he tried a little harder. He did this everyday for four weeks. It was at that point he realized what was ahead or what was not ahead.

The simple act of trying to lift himself out of the wheelchair spoke to him in ways that were profound and simple. My father in his dementia and pain learned what he needed to learn. He stopped eating. He turned away from me and the pretty nurses. He no longer spoke. He slept in the fetal position. He was aging backwards, edging toward the day when his breath would give out. He would be released.

I would be released from caring for him. He was leaving me a little more each day. If I were a math student, I might think of it in percentages, but I am not. He heard everything I said and everything the nurses said.

When Be Nice Bernice was dying, my father and I were talking about Barbra Streisand, my mother's favorite singer. In her morphine-induced slumber, she knew that we were talking about Barbra, and we were wrong in what we said about her: "You are both wrong." My father was in a twilight sleep. I told him I loved him. The morphine ensured that he would not have pain. I held his ancient hands that polished sparkly jewelry in his manufacturing factory. I held his hands that cradled me as an infant and fed me a bottle of milk when Be Nice Bernice, my mother, had surgery and wasn't able to hold me. I held the hands that slapped me when I was fresh. I held the hands that pulled me out of the Atlantic Ocean when a wave knocked me over. I held the hands that supported me when I lunged backward and he grabbed me. It was one of the favorite things we did together. I trusted those hands.

I held his hands and told him he could let go. He let go of my hands. He heard everything. His breathing was irregular. I reached out for his hands again and said goodbye before he was gone.

The nurses and aides loved him and were there with us. It was peaceful: noisy breathing, a cough, a sigh, and then no more. He died on January 30.

My father was cremated. Be Nice Bernice was cremated. I had my mother's remains in an urn. We combined their remains.

I found my father's *tallith*, or prayer shawl. It was worn by men at morning services and on *Yom Kippur*, the highest of holy days. My father's *tallith* was silk with blue and white stripes. It was knotted with a fringe on the four corners. I found Be Nice's white Bible with gold leaf on the binding. She held it in her hand when she married my father, as I did when I married Ron.

His grandchild, nieces and nephews visited with me in Cary. We held a memorial service for my father. We placed my parents' ashes in Bloomingdale shopping bags. You know, those ugly brown ones with the large 'B' on the side. We drove to the tennis courts near the clubhouse where I lived. My father was a passionate tennis player.

We brought the *tallith* and prayer book to the tennis courts. Thankfully, no one was playing tennis. We each read *kaddish* which was the prayer for the dead. Each one of us wore the *tallith* when we read our piece. We read it in English; we were reformed Jews. We did not need to hire a rabbi. We spoke the words from the tiny, dainty bride's prayer book. My father was the last person to wear his *tallith*. We wore it and honored him at his service. The prayer shawl had come full circle. We scattered the ashes in the small pond near the tennis courts.

Life was getting back to normal. The past year, normal was about my father. In some way, I missed the routine. There was no one to demand too much of me. I hoped no one would needle me the way he did. I thought about his life; he had a long one. He was successful in business without an education or connections.

I was able to see Dan more frequently. I unpacked, opened boxes, and reconnected with my favorite pieces of pottery. I slowly began to get my house in order. I received permission from the owner of the house, me, and moved into the master bedroom. I purchased a new bedroom set.

Spring occurred and I hadn't noticed. I was diligent in my unpacking. I worked hard with long days. I donated my father's clothes to Goodwill. I was moving in and my father's possessions were being disposed of.

Dan was planning a trip to California for us. He had a brother who lived there and a friend from Raleigh. I looked forward to a vacation. Dan officially retired from the EPA. He, too, had more free time.

We continued to attend performances at the ballet and symphony. We saw *Pink Martini* twice, once when they performed with the Raleigh symphony and another time at the Durham Performing Arts Center. We were busy, and I was enjoying my free time. I signed up for dance classes at the clubhouse. I made some friends.

Routines were re-established and the rhythm of life had returned. Dan wanted to spend more time with me. He again expressed his desire for marriage. I had hoped it was a phase and, like an adolescent, he would grow out of it.

I packed his clothes for the trip to California. He brought more clothing than I did. We were away for twelve days. In the years we were together, which wasn't quite two years, the most time we spent together consecutively was four days. We visited his brother and his family. We went to wineries and tasted wines at eleven a.m. I stopped after three tastings. Dan forgot to stop and was a silly drunk. We stopped for lunch. When you turned sixty-five, the national park system was free of charge, and Dan was sixty-five. A perk of aging, I guessed.

We went to Yosemite; there was fog on the windy roads up the mountain. Dan's brother was a terrific driver on those curvy roads. We saw maybe half a foot in front of us. The backup of cars reminded me of New York. I sat in the backseat. I had motion sickness. I told no one.

After a few hours, the fog disappeared but the rain did not. It drizzled on and off. The views of waterfalls and rock formations were incredible. I believed in God and national parks. People photographed sights and sounds of waterfalls and birds. The fresh smell of rainwater, trees so tall, I felt tiny and insignificant among this quiet humbling forest.

We drove back, and Tom, Dan's brother, dropped us off at the hotel. We had rented a car and left it at the hotel. Tom's wife, Sue, met us at the hotel and we all had dinner together. Tom was a semi-retired private detective. His young wife, his second or third, was not retired. I thanked him for his exceptional driving skills.

We had a nice evening to top off an interesting day. We said our goodbyes. The next day we visited with Dan's friend, Masuki. He was Japanese and Doug worked with him in Raleigh. We met for dinner, and after dinner we went to their house in the mountains in Glendale. Their children and grandchildren showed up. They were lovely; one daughter was a musician, and the other was an architect.

We went to LA. I dragged Dan to Melrose Avenue. We wondered

around the shops. I brought Dan to a Holocaust museum. My stepmother-in-law, Gerda, was interviewed by Steven Spielberg. We were able to hear her tell the story of her escape. It was in the movie *Voyage of the Damned*.

We went to the Beat Museum and heard Jack Kerouac speak in a short film. We viewed numerous photos of Allen Ginsburg and saw the 1949 Hudson that was used in the movie *On the Road*.

We headed out to San Francisco. We stopped in Malibu so Dan could tell everyone he was there. I have always loved San Francisco, and we stayed there for four or five nights. We took a boat ride to Sausalito, the same one Ron and I took a thousand years ago in my other life. We went to Chinatown. It was great, blocks and blocks of street vendors. We drove toward Pacific Palisades and took pictures of the Victorian homes.

The trip was winding down. We were leaving the next day. I packed most of our clothing. I was tired and wanted to nap. I asked Dan if he would take a walk or get a cup of tea. He was upset.

"You don't want me here." I said I wanted to rest. I told him he was making noise, and I just needed forty-five minutes of quiet. He was offended. I was tired, plain and simple. He left but was annoyed with me. I needed alone time.

I never slept, but I thought about my life. By and large, the trip had been pleasant enough. It was good to get away. Dan would take it personally if I said I wanted to be alone for an afternoon. He turned it around and said, "You don't want to be with me." He did that a lot. He took it personally when it was not meant to be.

Dan had a sweetness that would be irreplaceable. He had a generosity of heart. He made me a better and kinder person; his kindness was honest and innocent. I believed my father had better care because Dan was in my life. I was not ready for marriage. I would never be ready. Our timing was off. After Dan's wife died, he was ready.

On the plane ride home, I knew it was not meant to be. It was close to our second year together, and I wanted to end it before he bought me another lovely present. I was sad; I knew it would be painful for both of us, but it was over. I decided to tell him soon after we were home in Cary. I knew I would never meet anyone as sweet as him.

I decided to stop dating. I would never be ready. If Ron waltzed back into my life, I would not be ready. That was not true. I would be ready again and again, of course, he would be healthy. Adam mentioned what a nice life Ron and I would have had, if he had lived. I never thought about that. I had not realized how astute Adam was.

Most of the men that I had dated married after our relationship ended. One became a Buddhist monk. Dan married a woman soon after me, Stewart as well. I was happy for Dan; he deserved the best. I spoke with him and wished him happiness.

I've discovered that I've had more success in real estate than in love. My love line was short, and I am short. My palm told the short story. When reading palms, the hand that you write with is not the palm that is read. My right palm was read.

I became more involved in my community. I took cardio and dance classes. I met women and went to lunch and dinner with friends. We took shopping trips. I missed the comfort and ease of female companionship.

I joined the monthly writers' group. It was a slow entry back into the world of words. It was an informal group that met for two hours, once a month. There was a roving cast of characters, but there was a basic core. It was fine.

My birthday was fast approaching. I was turning sixty-five and some friends were taking me out to lunch. I noticed in the local paper that there was a writers' conference about ten minutes from my home. I gave myself the North Carolina Writers' Network Fall Conference as a birthday present. I turned sixty-five on Nov 2. The conference was that weekend. Friday night was a meet and greet with book displays and wandering writers everywhere. I signed up for two workshops, one on memoir writing and another on playwriting. On Saturday, there was a guest writer, Edith Pearlman, who wrote a collection of short stories called *Binocular Vision.* There were editors, agents, and publishers. In the evening, we had dinner and entertainment. I signed up for the open mic on Saturday evening after the music. We were allowed to read for five minutes.

12
WRIST FRACTURES

❦

On November 5th, I fractured my wrist, or did I break it? You break up with your boyfriend, your car breaks down, and you are broke. You want to break your spouse's neck...why do you break up with someone then, after the break up you break down?

The fact was I fractured my wrist at the dermatologist's office. I am left-handed but right brain prone. I broke it in five places and required surgery. I went to occupational therapy. I needed a new occupation. I was retired. I needed a new line of work. I wanted a new way to play, minus the fracturing part. This was not the first bone that I broke. I might have broken almost all of my toes.

The most memorable break was in Waldbaums, a grocery store chain in New York. I was strolling down the peanut butter aisle. This was the late 80s; I remember all things unimportant because that was my job. Peanut butter was not housed in those light plastic containers that are polluting landfills and sewers today.

I gingerly picked up the glass Jiffy jar of peanut butter. It fell on my toe, the toe next to the big toe. I moaned and whimpered; people walked right past me as if I was invisible. Perhaps I was too quiet in my whimpering because I was a wimp. The other breaks were from ballet and painting the bathroom ceiling.

I broke my pinky toe, and that was the funniest of all, since the toe separated from the other toes as if it was no longer a member of that foot. I learned how to mend it without sitting in the doctor's office. You simply tape the toe next to the broken toe and hope for the best.

This is not like the foot bindings performed on young children in China. The children's toes were broken intentionally. This was done so the child would have small feet. She would then be able to marry into a prosperous family. They hobbled about, while their toes healed. Foot binding was abolished in 1911. American women were allowed to vote in the USA in 1920.

My fractured wrist was healing. I was a good healer. I was writing on the computer with my right hand. After attending the North Carolina Writers' Network Conference in Cary, I made a commitment to myself to write five pages a day and then I fell, but I am still committed. I have learned that left-handed people are accident prone; they don't live to be ninety. That was never an aspiration of mine.

When I read my piece at the Conference's open mic, I felt like I was doing standup. I enjoyed sharing my words in front of an audience. I loved hearing the words and stories of others. My reading was a far cry from the time I read in Southampton, *"My Last Pill and Testament."* There were no tears. Sunday morning at the conference was for goodbyes.

Ron's death taught me how to live. It taught me how to live a fuller life. I discovered that I was stronger than I or anyone thought I was. My sense of humor keeps me balanced and off balance. Writing groups and film groups are powerful. There will always be another workshop, another book to read, a film to view, a place to visit, a friend to meet, or a day at the beach. I called Ron's friends on our anniversary, August 8. I am not sure why that's the day I called. I caught up with them to see how they were doing. They didn't call me back, but that was OK. I know I will keep in touch with them.

I missed my friends from Florida. I rented a small apartment in Sarasota within walking distance of some of my friends. I prayed that they remain healthy so we can grow old and better together.

I found out what happened to my old, two-bedroom apartment with a view of Sarasota Bay and the sunset. The owner, Patty, whose husband was incarcerated, died in 2011. The apartment was sold in 2012.

I hired a real estate broker. She showed me lots of properties. I was weary as usual. I hoped to find a home to shelter me from the cold. A home closer to the equator that would warm and shower me with longer days.

I take my commitment to write quite seriously. I brought my sloppy pages to Ronda. She immediately explained the value of having a folder. She was a treasure. She calls herself a book midwife, and, indeed, she was. The first draft of my memoir was completed in nine months, and I met my editor, Alice Osborn, at last year's North Carolina Writers' Network fall conference in Wrightsville Beach, North Carolina. Besides being an editor and writing coach, Alice is on the board and facilitating a women's writing retreat in August in Marshall, near Asheville, my old stomping grounds. I registered as soon as I found out. I understand there will be organic food, so I might have to sneak in some Diet Pepsi. Who said you can't go home again?

Shortly after Ron's death, I visited a psychic/channeler. He told me that

Ron wanted me to hurry up and finish the book. I never told the psychic I was writing a book. He saw Ron and I dancing as we did at weddings and parties. Ron was no longer in pain and wanted me to go on with my life. I cried salty tears. In my future, I see essays, poetry and perhaps a short story. There is talk of a collaboration with a friend on a non-fiction project . . . we shall see.

I am not fickle about writing but I am fickle about the quality of my writing.

There is a question I ask my friends and acquaintances: "If you could live your life over again, would you?" However, you would have to live it exactly the way it was the first time around. It would be identical, and you would know exactly how it would play out. You cannot change anything. Would you live it again?

> *To Ron:*
> *What if it was me who left you?*
> *What if it was my kidneys that were flunking life with a D?*
> *What if it my heart was enlarged and required a replacement?*
> *What if there were no ifs? Would you care? Would you dare?*
> *Would you do what I could not?*
> *Would you be four seconds away from not caring?*
> *Would you dose me the morphine to ease my days into nights*
> *of dumb into a phantasmagoric finale?*
> *Would you do what I could not?*
> *Would you do it better?*

There were days when I was seconds away from not caring, but I continued to care. When my own body was dying in its own perfect way, cells were multiplying with me not noticing.

To Ron continues:

Who cared?
There were days I wished your suffering to cease.
A young cardiologist told us that "Our job is to do no harm."
Yet harm was done to you, to others.
I don't visit your gravesite.
Adam put stones on your headstone.
Both Adam and I have photographed your gravesite.
I think you would be pleased.
We did not put the Ten Commandments on the stone.
We had the scales of Lady Justice engraved.

Be Nice Bernice cared for her mother, my grandmother, May. My mother had two older sisters. Be Nice was twelve years younger than her oldest sister and eight years younger than the middle one. Be Nice was the change of life child. I find that expression interesting. The change, better known as menopause, is all about the moon. I think it is the baby that changes the life whether the child is planned or not. My grandmother didn't know she was pregnant until the very end. Be Nice, my mother, adored her father, David; my middle name is Davie or Dayvie. I suppose in some way when my grandmother became a widow at fifty-five, my mother was a little like a widow as well. My grandfather owned a delicatessen on the east side of Manhattan. Be Nice and my grandparents worked in the store in shifts. When David died, I think the deli died with him. Be Nice and my grandmother would not be able to keep it afloat. They never tried; they moved to Jackson Heights in a one-bedroom apartment to be near Ruth, the oldest daughter. Ruth lived with her husband and children. Be Nice wanted to be a journalist; she was not married. She was shy and hated dentists. When Be Nice was in school, she forged a document that said she had been seen by a dentist. She must have gotten hell for that. She hungered to be with her father. He was her idol. I know nothing about him. I have photos where I noticed his Hungarian good looks. I suppose it was understood that my mother would be the caregiver. It usually is the female child, but there were only females. Be Nice's sister visited with their mother, but, truly, Grandma was my mother's to have and to hold. They shared the one bedroom.

For the part of the family history that I am not able to recreate or remember, I have the family photos as a tool. The day after I reluctantly married, Be Nice deposited all the photos into my questionable hands. She tossed them to me as if a burden was lifted and I should possess that burden. She was granted relief, perhaps it is a tradition. I am feeling that way toward Adam. If he were married, I would wrap them up and present them to him. You are the one, Adam, you piece it together.

The photos of my mother were striking. Be Nice was wearing a fur coat, two or three different ones. One was Mouton and another was Persian lamb. My father told me that Grandma paid for them every month for Be Nice. My father told me he inherited those bills when he married my mother. I guess that was fair. The three of them lived in a one-bedroom apartment. My grandmother gave my parents the bedroom, and she slept on the couch in the living room. The couch she slept upon was brocade velvet, not midnight blue, with removable doilies on the arms of the couch. I am recalling all of this from black-and-white photographs and my childhood memories when I lived in that apartment. Thank you, Mom, for handing them over to me.

Be Nice died three months before Ron. My father came up from Florida to Westhampton after Be Nice died. He was eighty-two. He looked fifteen years younger. We drove together to visit Ron at St. Luke's Hospital. My father weathered the cold weather pretty well. He lived in Florida for close to thirty years. He would park my car for me, and I would rush to see Ron not making any progress. I never grew accustomed to my father's humming, singing, tapping, and whistling in the car.

When Adam was ill, I was not speaking with my parents. We did reconnect and Be Nice asked me why I didn't tell her about Adam and his illness.

"I was scared of you, Mom, always. I loved you, and I was petrified of you. You would call me at five a.m. to tell me you would hate me for the rest of your life."

13
THE LAST COUCH

Couché in French means to lie down in. In Turkish, a sofa is a long, stuffed seat for reclining. In Aramaic it is a suffah. A couch turkey is a psychiatrist.

After Ron's stroke, he would use his outside voice to yell, "Chair Nurse!" until a nurse came in to see how he was. Ron simply wanted to get out of the reclining chair that they wanted him to sit in. He was not able to buzz the buzzer for the nurse. His voice now was his strongest asset. Ron never raised his voice before the stroke. He was shocked when I told him he was an attorney.

A couch is a couch. It is where one can read, watch a film, and take an accidental nap. You can eat a potato and become a couch potato. This is my last couch. It was born in 1979. We moved into our first home in

Lawrence, New York. We went to Bloomingdales in New York. We were taken back by the prices but then I saw her.

She was modular with curvy, round arms and full of art deco glamour. You could have her placed in the shape it was intended; that would be in the shape of an 'L.' You could separate them, and one would be a free-standing chaise lounge. I loved the flexibility; it catered to my fickleness.

I cancelled the wedding three times. I liked the bride part. I slept one hour the night before the wedding. I bit the inside of my lip, as I was known to do when I was nervous. I told Be Nice Bernice, my mother, that I was not attending the wedding.

She looked at me and through me. "We are ready. You will get dressed and be a bride." She did not mention the wife part.

The couch has had some work done. She has been repaired and recovered. She is on her third fabric. Her first fabric that we chose in the store was a sand pebble color. Her second was a bold black with a charcoal gray alternating stripe.

She resided in Westhampton, New York, where we moved when Ron became ill. After five years, no more surgeries or repairs. I remained there for five years, after he left.

I lived in Cary, North Carolina, in a retirement community for over three years. I am sixty-six years old and you remain fifty-seven, as this is a forever couch.

The third and last fabric on the couch is a zebra print. I loved it. I love it. I don't know if Ron would have liked it. She has been living in her zebra skin for the past two years. She is thirty-four. Our son is thirty-nine.

I am thinking, if I stay healthy, that there might be a fourth fabric, a brown-and-white cow print. A southwest look, perhaps. I love her as much as when I first met her, maybe more. She has been transformed; she has traveled. She has lived in many locations. She has weathered many storms. She has witnessed many parties and accidental naps. She is forever evolving.

The chameleon couch made it to home plate. Home is where the dishes are.

Weddings rock at home

Midwives deliver perfect and imperfect newborns at . . .

Accidents frequently happen at. . .

People commit suicide at . . .

People travel the world to purchase memories to bring back...

Home is where I listen to Edith Piaf and Dave Matthews.

Home is where I sign a simple lease that permits me to spend a couple of months in

Someone else's . . .

I bring my photographs. I like them with me.

My family history in black and white.

I had my wedding pictures decolorized.

pay close attention to the various apartments I have lived in.

I lived in different apartments that were situated near every subway stop

Of the E line in Queens County, New York.

We moved every three years when the lease was up rather than remove

Everything from the wall and let the painter's paint.

We packed our belongings or maybe just our longings.

A friend asked me how I felt about the constant moving; the truth was

I didn't think about it much.

I assumed everyone lived like that.

Except for my cousins who lived in a real house not an apartment that had

More than one floor and you had to buy it, then you lived there forever unless

Someone died or there was a hurricane.

Always seek higher ground in disaster or in life if you can if you care.

The Last Couch

www.ingramcontent.com/pod-product-compliance
Lightning Source LLC
LaVergne TN
LVHW011224080426
835509LV00005B/300